The Legen

LLANDWROG

The story of an airfield and the birth of the RAF Mountain Rescue Service

Edward Doylerush

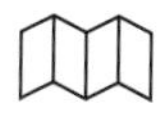

Midland Counties Publications

Contents

First Published in 1994 by
Midland Counties Publications
24 The Hollow, Earl Shilton, Leicester
LE9 7NA, England.

ISBN 0 904597 88 1

Printed and bound by
Woolnough Bookbinding Limited
Irthlingborough, Northants.
NN9 5SE

Front cover photograph: See page 34
Back cover photograph: The airfield in 1978

DEDICATION

This work is dedicated to all personnel who served or trained at RAF stations Llandwrog, Penrhos, Hell's Mouth and, in particular, to those who lost their lives during that period, or when they later served on operational squadrons. Also to the members of the Llandwrog Mountain Rescue Team, who snatched many lives from Snowdonia's peaks.

Foreword
by
The Rt Hon Lord Cledwyn of Penrhos PC, CH

Those who served in one of the three services in the 1939-45 War look back on those years with varied feelings and memories. In many cases the memories are vivid because of their grimness whilst others have faded with the passage of time. We remember those fellow servicemen and women with whom we lived and worked. They became close and valued friends over a comparatively short period, but half a century has passed and they too are memories today.

Two men called at our home recently and as my wife greeted them, one asked 'Does Hughie live here?' Hughes became Hughie very quickly in the RAF of fifty years ago. I was delighted to see these two old RAF friends and we spent a happy evening together.

In this imaginative and carefully researched book, Edward Doylerush has brought to life the wartime activities of RAF Llandwrog. In addition to its normal flying operations, which it shared with other small stations in the vicinity, Llandwrog made its name as the pioneer RAF Mountain Rescue Service and became the model for today's important Service of which RAF Valley in Anglesey, with its famous Rescue Helicopter Unit, not far from Llandwrog, is a proud example.

Flying the Ansons, the Halifaxes, the Wellingtons, and other aircraft over and between the mountains of Snowdonia in those crucial days called for skill and steady nerves, and these qualities were also needed by those operating the Rescue Service. The author has succeeded in conveying the courage and dedication of the young men who were involved in these perilous operations. The book is made the more readable by the wealth of personal experience and anecdote which have been brought together here.

I had the privilege of serving in Llandwrog for a short time in 1945 and came to know many of the aircrew and mountain rescue personnel. My admiration for them has not faded and I am grateful to Edward Doylerush for this memorable account of their achievements and qualities.

House of Lords,
1994

Unmistakable outline of an Avro Anson over Conway Police Station in 1941, just as a bomb is let off in a mock air raid.
North Wales Weekly News

Preface and Acknowledgements

This is the story of three inter-related Royal Air Force stations situated in north-west Wales. The first, Penrhos, was a pre-war grass airfield, with its 'baby', the tiny landing ground with bombing and gunnery range at Hell's Mouth. The third, Llandwrog, which is the main theme of this work, with tarmac runways and large accommodation and facilities started as a satellite of Penrhos, but gradually overshadowed the latter until their roles were reversed. Their lives were so inter-woven that some mention must be made of their mutual impact and activities. Not only that but, from Llandwrog emerged the model of the RAF Mountain Rescue Service which has been developed into the celebrated service of today. Indeed, this work is being published in the fiftieth year that the Service came formally into being.

Each region of wartime Britain had its own 'flying flavour'. In the south east of Britain were mainly fighter airfields, initially for defence, but later to include offensive roles. East Anglia and Lincolnshire was known as 'bomber country', with RAF squadrons active mainly through the night and USAAF squadrons usually throughout the daylight hours from the summer of 1942. Certainly these regions held no place for training aircraft. Airfields for these sprang up along the western seaboard, North Wales included. The cross country (and over sea) flights would be made by Ansons from Penrhos, and Llandwrog, when operated as an Observers Advanced Flying Unit, and later from No.8(O)AFU at Mona. Often they would make their morning constitutional runs towards a turning point at Rhyl, or Point of Ayr. At Rhos-on-Sea where the writer, a keen Air Training Corps cadet, lived at the time, Ansons would roar above the rooftops so low that the serial numbers could be easily read, including a batch in 1944/45 being LT980-LT989. Later in the day they returned at a higher altitude, ragged and tired looking. At weekends I would try to log the return of most of the outgoing aircraft, if returning along the coast, with a telescope trained on them. It would be many years on that I would discover that some not so recorded had been lost in the mountains or had come down in the sea. There was always wooden aircraft wreckage being washed up on the beach in those days. Only the size of the tragedy was not then known.

I have been fortunate to make contact with some of the personnel who served or trained at Llandwrog, who shared their experiences with me. Also, with those who were part of the growing team of rescuers endeavouring to save a few lives from the many mountain crashes.

It may seem strange, but a civilian was of more value in the field of welfare than half a dozen entertainments officers. Mrs Mary Williams, with her husband Hugh, lived at Rhydfelen, a small farmhouse situated alongside the airfield. Here, on cold frosty days, she produced for hungry airmen ham and eggs, or delicious cheese on toast, the latter for one penny, all washed down with a mug of tea in front of the open range. No one questioned where all the food came from. Even with rationing, there was no real shortage in this rural retreat. The many airmen who served here, groundstaff and flyers alike, recall her welcome with affection.

Of all the airfields in the area, Llandwrog holds a special place for the writer. As I researched the stories of the mountain crashes for my first book 'No Landing Place', the name of that airfield and airmen who flew from it kept arising. I climbed to little known crash sites where RAF, Commonwealth, and Allied airmen perished, their names etched on my memory. I would say a few words to their unseen spirits that they would not be forgotten, and this work is part of their story. Readers will find more detailed stories of some of the incidents in the earlier work.

In the '60s my family and I spent many happy hours on the beach at Dinas Dinlle before I learned something of the then almost derelict airfield close by. I went back on my own one day when civil flying had just started. I took a little used path from the camp along the Foryd shore, turning inland up a track by a derelict machine gun post. Suddenly the control tower and windsock revealed themselves against an evening sky. It seemed for an instant in time as if the airfield of wartime might come alive again to the roar of Whitleys or Ansons taking off. If a little of that atmosphere has been captured and passed on to the reader, then I have succeeded in my task.

Wales has been left a bounty of legends. Perhaps in some future era a little of the history and stories of the wartime airfield will be weaved into them – the Legend of Llandwrog. For the sake of continuity, Welsh place names in the text are generally used as they appeared on the maps and official documents of the time. Any correspondence will be welcomed by the author.

Acknowledgements
My grateful thanks to all the ex-airmen, and ground staff, and former members of the Llandwrog RAF Mountain Rescue Team, who co-operated so wholeheartedly and without whose help this work would not have come to fruition. There are too many to thank all individually, but their names appear in the various chapters. In addition, my special thanks to Lord Cledwyn of Penrhos for taking valuable time off to contribute a foreword. Also, Air Historical Branch, MOD., Arthur Arculus for New Zealand research, Charles & Rowan Birch in Canada for fine efforts in tracing Wally Prosser's relatives, Chaz Bowyer, the Commonwealth War Graves Commission, the librarians of Conwy

Hugh and Mary Williams outside Rhydfelen, their 'cafe' near the airfield.
O M Williams (son)

Library for locating research material, Ken Coward, Alan Davie for 312 (Czech) Squadron photographs, Glyn Davies again, for all the photographic copying, Arthur Evans, Aldon P. Ferguson, Glyn & Pat Griffith, Evan L. Jones in Leopold, Australia, who did not live to see his contributions appear, Gordon Leigh whose fine wartime photographs are reproduced and who also did not live to see the outcome of our friendship, I shall always treasure our visit together to his old base in 1991, Mrs C. M. Liddiard, for Tom Yates' photographs, J. L. Poole, historian Bob Roberts, who lived at Pwllheli and whose father Ted served in the RAF Marine Unit there, and later at Llandwrog, David Roberts, the late Miss Hope Roberts, Dr. Tom Scudamore, David J. Smith, Denis J. Travis who gave me so much invaluable material from fourteen months spent at Penrhos and Llandwrog, Mr O. M. Williams, formerly of Rhydfelen, and to my wife, Mary, who waits for the garden to be rescued.

Edward Doylerush,
Snowdonia, 1994

Warning

Some of the mountainous areas are remote and dangerous, especially in winter. Cliffs, scree and boggy areas should be avoided. If one is not experienced in mountain walking, travel with someone who is, and only proceed if the weather forecast is fair and without mist. Take adequate warm and water proof clothing, O.S. map, compass, torch, first aid kit, whistle, food, and survival bag. Should the weather start to deteriorate – TURN BACK.

Leave word behind of your route and stick to it, with an expected return time incorporating plenty of time for the walk, exploration and a margin. Naismith's Rule states that an hour to traverse 3 map miles, with an extra half an hour for every 1,000 feet of ascent.

Aircraft Wreckage

The remains of crashed British, German, and United States military aircraft are the responsibility of the Ministry of Defence. Recovery of parts may not be carried out without the permission of the MoD. Human remains, bombs, and live ammunition may still be at sites. Contact point for recovery groups is: Ministry of Defence, S10s(Air), Room 607, Adastral House, Theobalds Road, London WC1X 8RU.

Air Atlantique's DH.89A Rapide G-AIDL (ex-RAF TX310) at Caernarfon Airport. Author and grandchildren in picnic area.
Mary Doylerush

Part I

Airfields and Airmen

312 Squadron Hurricane V6878 'DU-L' at readiness at Penrhos.
via Alan Davie

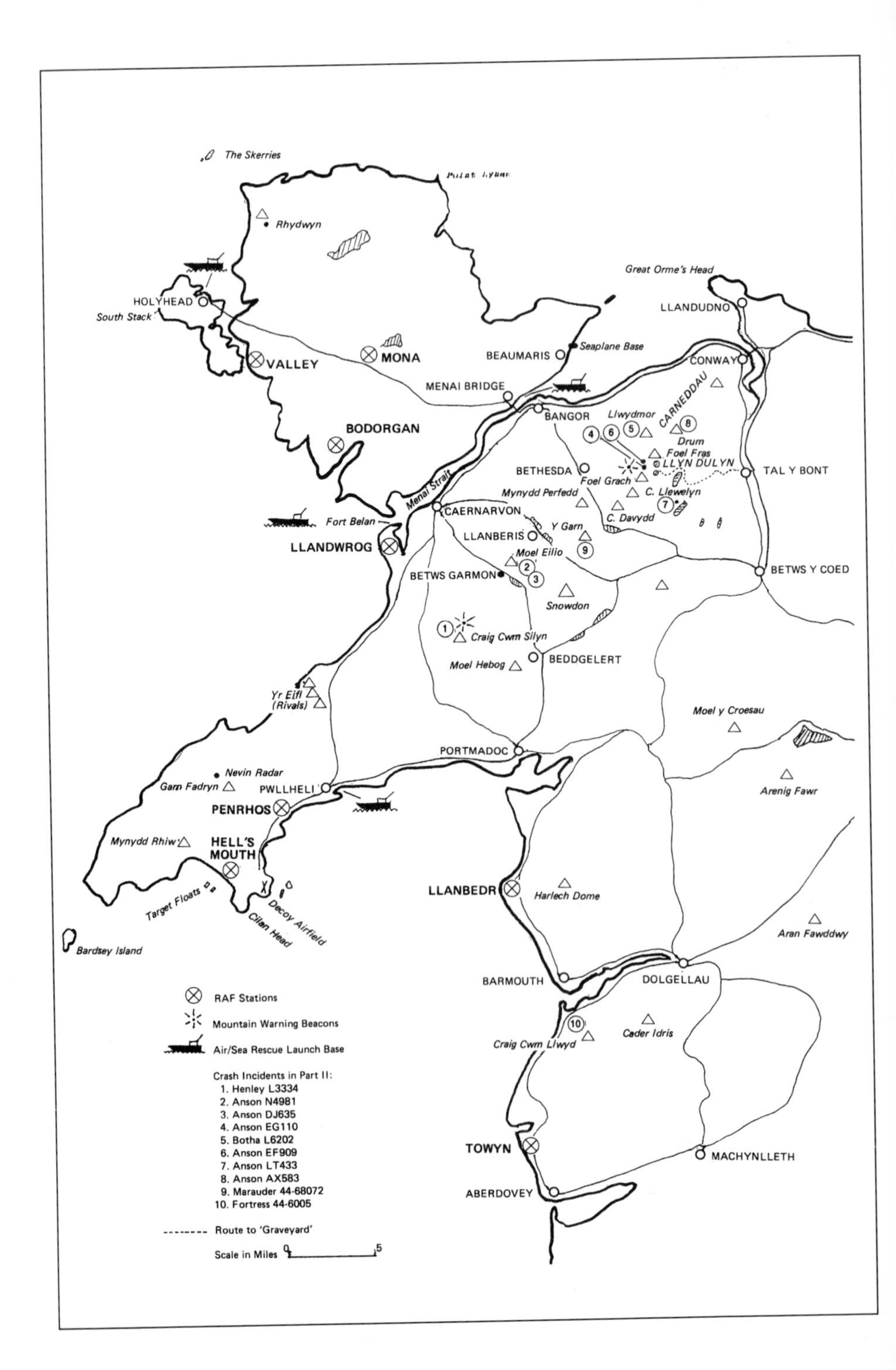
The Skerries
Rhydwyn
HOLYHEAD
South Stack
VALLEY
MONA
BODORGAN
BEAUMARIS
Seaplane Base
MENAI BRIDGE
Great Orme's Head
LLANDUDNO
CONWAY
CARNEDDAU
BANGOR
Llwydmor
Drum
Foel Fras
LLYN DULYN
BETHESDA
Foel Grach
C. Llewelyn
TAL Y BONT
Mynydd Perfedd
C. Davydd
Menai Strait
CAERNARVON
Fort Belan
LLANDWROG
LLANBERIS
Y Garn
Moel Eilio
BETWS GARMON
Snowdon
BETWS Y COED
Craig Cwm Silyn
Moel Hebog
BEDDGELERT
Yr Eifl (Rivals)
Moel y Croesau
PORTMADOC
Nevin Radar
Garn Fadryn
PWLLHELI
PENRHOS
Arenig Fawr
Mynydd Rhiw
HELL'S MOUTH
Target Floats
Cilan Head
Decoy Airfield
LLANBEDR
Harlech Dome
Bardsey Island
Aran Fawddwy
BARMOUTH
DOLGELLAU
Cader Idris
Craig Cwm Llwyd
TOWYN
MACHYNLLETH
ABERDOVEY
RAF Stations
Mountain Warning Beacons
Air/Sea Rescue Launch Base
Crash Incidents in Part II:
1. Henley L3334
2. Anson N4981
3. Anson DJ635
4. Anson EG110
5. Botha L6202
6. Anson EF909
7. Anson LT433
8. Anson AX583
9. Marauder 44-68072
10. Fortress 44-6005
Route to 'Graveyard'
Scale in Miles 0 5

Chapter One

RAF Penrhos & Hell's Mouth

RAF PENRHOS

With the expansion of the RAF, in January 1936 the Air Ministry concluded the purchase of a farm of 250 acres near Pwllheli, and seven farms bordering the bay of Porth Neigwl (Hell's Mouth) near the southern tip of the Lleyn Peninsula. A lease was also obtained of the foreshore between Mynydd Rhiw and Cilan Head for target facilities. The contract, provisionally set at £250,000 for the construction work, was awarded to Howeson Ltd of Glasgow.

While the contract provided much needed work for the local labour force, Welsh Nationalists objected to a military aerodrome here, a possible target in any future war. On the night of 8th September 1936, three of their number, led by Saunders Lewis, set fire to contractors offices, and stores, which action put a hundred men out of work. Not only that, but the subsequent publicity from the trial held at the Old Bailey placed Penrhos high on the list of prospective targets for the Luftwaffe.

RAF Penrhos opened on 1st February 1937, as No.5 Armament Training Camp, under the command of Wing Commander T.V.Lister, with a complement of Westland Wallace biplanes. The site was not ideal for anything larger than the single engined biplanes, for the grass surface airfield was saucer shaped, with the hazard of a ridge in excess of 100 feet behind the huts on the northwest perimeter. There was also an unwelcome drop of over twenty feet on the south west perimeter, where several twin engined aircraft went over the edge on landing into the prevailing wind, unable to stop because of the short runway available (2,300 feet compared to the shortest at Llandwrog of 3,200 feet), and often wet grass. Many camp buildings also were too close for comfort.

A Marine Section, No.51 Air Sea Rescue Base was established in Pwllheli harbour with five locally built patrol pinnaces to maintain the target floats in Hell's Mouth Bay, and keep shipping out of the area when the bombing range was in use. Indeed two boats were armoured as target boats for smoke bombs. Live bombs were only used outside the three mile limit under stringent precautions; a safety officer would always be on duty in a tower at Hell's Mouth to oversee proceedings. The pinnaces were also useful in providing a rescue service for airmen unfortunate enough to ditch in the locality, though this was not their prime purpose. A boat shed with slipway was erected, (This still stands, owned at the time of writing by Partington Marine) with the crews and maintenance staff for the base being accommodated in part of the Victoria Hotel on Pwllheli promenade.

The first training course started on 3rd April 1937, when thirty four aircraft from No.10 FTS at Tern Hill flew in. These four week courses kept the staff busy until the outbreak of war. One of the first staff pilots to arrive in March 1937 was Sergeant George Blagden who informs us that trainee pilots would first fire the fixed forward guns of their aircraft, to be followed by exercises from the Lewis gun in the rear cockpit so that they would have a better appreciation of air gunners' problems. He notes 'Three types of target were used from the Wallace, the flag (or banner), the sleeve, and the cone. The flag was about 12 x 60 feet, stiffened by a pole at the leading edge and flown some 3,400 yards

Penrhos Airfield in 1937. Westland Wallaces and uncompleted hangar. *Bob Roberts*

RAF Penrhos vertical, 14th August 1945. *RAF photograph, Crown Copyright.*

behind the aircraft. They were held in containers each side of the fuselage until deployed. After the firing attacks, the flags were dropped on the airfield at Hell's Mouth for assessment of accuracy from the colour tipped bullets used by different aircraft.' By September 1939 the Wallaces started to be replaced by Hawker Henleys and Fairey Battles. Blagden was allocated to 'B' Flight flying the Battles. These were used both for air to air and air to ground firing, and for bombing exercises. At this time several ungainly looking Harrow bombers were allocated to Penrhos. George Blagden: 'On September 8th I was driving to Penrhos with my wife when she exclaimed 'Is that aeroplane alright?". I glanced round and saw a Harrow climbing at a steep angle, almost at stalling speed. The port wing dropped and it fell in a slow, flat spiral until it hit the ground, exploding with a roar and flash, flames and smoke pouring into the air. I told my wife to stay in the car and rushed to the scene. I was concerned about the crew and the fact that a summer camp for boys had been established in the field. Indeed some of the boys were running towards the crash. I shouted for them to keep away. One of them shouted 'There is one of them down there, Mister". I cleared the low hedge wire and stream to reach the airman lying beside the wreck, recognising him as Sergeant L.J.Hilton, and that he would have been flying solo with an unarmed aircraft. At this point one of the boys arrived and helped me move the pilot up the steep bank to a less vulnerable position. Hilton sustained two broken legs and a broken arm, but eventually returned to flying. I learned later that an engine failure forced Hilton to turn away from a straight ahead landing because of the boys' camp, and ending up in the rough terrain that he did.' On 3rd September 1939 Penrhos changed its role to become No.9 Air Observers School, but on 1st November it changed again to become No.9 Bombing and Gunnery School. The few Wallaces left,

Penrhos ground crew with Westland Wallace. *Bob Roberts*

Pwllheli based RAF Pinnace. *Bob Roberts*

RAF Marine Section crew at Pwllheli. Corporal Ted Roberts on the right. *Bob Roberts*

Anson K6197 'R' of 220 Squadron, crashed off Penrhos airfield 17th September 1937. *Bob Roberts*

Fairey Battle N2026, of 12 OTU, crashed near Penrhos on 24th May 1940. The crew of three survived. *Tom Yates*

Pilots of 312 Czech Squadron doze in the winter sunshine while on standby. F/O Jan Cermak 2nd right. *via Alan Davie*

along with Henleys and Battles were used for target towing, with air gunner pupils seated in the Whitleys, Blenheims and Ansons.

From the previous unwanted publicity, Penrhos was one of the first airfields in the northwest to be attacked via the 'back door' of overrun French airfields. As the personnel accommodation had been built on the edge of the airfield, with no thought of dispersal, this was to have dire consequences. On 9th July 1940 a single Dornier Do 17 bombed the camp with deadly accuracy. George Blagden: 'I had recently been commissioned and about twenty officers were in the anteroom when the first bomb hit the sleeping quarters. The wooden buildings swayed and vibrated, a vase on the table disintegrated. Most people dropped to the floor, but quickly recovered from the shock, grabbed their helmets and gas masks and headed for their respective duties. I ran from the Mess down towards the main road where I was responsible for the gun post there. I found that none had fired a single shot. The crew said that they did not recognise the aircraft but it appeared to be coming in to land. They were not trained in gunnery or aircraft recognition, this was just an extra duty for them. Their surprise was complete'. Three blocks of officers quarters were demolished, two Henleys wrecked, a hangar badly damaged, and two officers killed, Flying Officer B.Page, and Pilot Officer G.D.Goldsmith Jones, a Canadian in the RAF who was visiting to carry out flying checks, and due to leave that day. He is buried in Denio Cemetery, Pwllheli, with many other service fatalities from the area.

Further attacks were made on 2nd, 3rd, 4th, 9th, and 10th October, with considerable damage being caused on a few days, and five casualties on the 2nd, though no further fatalities. These raids resulted in a flight of Spitfires from No.611 Squadron at Tern Hill arriving to protect the airfield. In December they were relieved by 'B' Flight of Hurricanes from No.312 (Czech) Squadron at Speke. These stayed through the severe winter of heavy snows on a peninsula which normally enjoys mild winters. Many patrols were flown over the sea endeavouring to catch a glimpse of the enemy, but the weather, and lack of radar, aided the Luftwaffe crews. It was not until 14th March 1941, that the

squadron CO, Flight Lieutenant Alex W.Dawbarn and Sergeant Joseph Stehlik were on patrol when they sighted a lone Junkers Ju 88 below them at 8,000 feet heading southeast for home. Dawbarn made the first attack from 200 yards, stopping its port engine. Stehlik then shot up the starboard engine from 100 yards, and repeated beam attacks were made in spite of heavy return fire until the attackers were out of ammunition. However the damage was done and the Junkers hit the sea 25 miles south west of Bardsey Island at 1127 hours. A dinghy and one crewman surfaced for a few seconds before sinking. While the identity of this aircraft is not known for certain, it was most likely 'VB+KJ' Werke No.0382, of 2nd Staffel AufMarinesgruppe Oberbefehslaken, with pilot Leutnant Fritz Thoms and three crew aboard, which did not return to its Le Bourget base after a reconnaissance trip to Glasgow. Sadly though, Dawbarn was reported missing on patrol on 10th April, presumed lost to the guns of an enemy aircraft. Later that month the Czechs moved on to RAF Valley, their presence having been a great comfort.

Penrhos was renamed No.9 Air Observers School again on 14th June 1941 to give observers a navigation course spiced with armament training. The gunnery training was transferred to Llandwrog which opened a few weeks later on 7th July. Stan Ascough passed out as wireless operator at Yatesbury and was one of twenty posted to Penrhos, awaiting his air gunners course, from 19th August to 25th November 1941. 'Flight Sergeant Jock Campbell DFM was in charge of us, and we flew in Ansons and Blenheims as wireless operators for the training of air observers. I remember my first Blenheim flight like yesterday. Sat on a bicycle-type seat facing the tail, no guns fitted, with the receiver at one side and the transmitter the other. Hell of a draught and bitterly cold. There was no intercom and the signal for the W/Op to go forward was for the pilot to wag the tail three times. Then had to crawl

Hurricanes Is 'DU-L' (V6878) and 'DU-S' of 312 Squadron, at readiness at Penrhos in early 1941. *via Alan Davie*

312 Squadron Hurricane V7028 'DU-V' refuelling from a bowser. *via Alan Davie*

Hurricane V7028 'DU-V', flown by Flying Officer Jan Cermak, after a forced landing in the Eigiau valley. *Tom Yates*

Sergeant Joseph Stehlik, of 312 Czech Squadron. *via Alan Davie*

Crashed Hurricane P3612 'DU-N', was a result of a collision on 22nd February 1941 at Penrhos. *Bob Roberts*

Three pilots of 312 Squadron scramble. Left to right: Sgt Svetlik, F/Lt Vasatko and F/Lt Alex Dawbarn, the C.O. *via Alan Davie*

Main hangar at Penhros with airfield and Llanbedrog Head in view. *George Blagen*

Airfield and Llanbedrog Head in view with caravans in1993.

RAF Hell's Mouth vertical. Camp mid-top, Four hangars on right, and moving target range between them and the sea.
RAF photograph, Crown copyright

Luftwaffe reconnaissance photograph taken on the 14th August 1940. The airfield and hangars are enclosed in a black line.
Bob Roberts

through the aircraft, get the message and crawl back again. Once, the down draught over the mountains was so bad that the transmitter crashed to the floor. It was quite a job carrying all the gear out to the aircraft in the morning, IFF set, six 2 volt accumulators, and a parachute. We were issued with three pairs of silk gloves and wool and leather gauntlets which made key bashing difficult, and two flying suits to help keep us warm. The only training I had on that first flight was from the senior man, AC2 Whittaker. He was lost with his entire crew of five, two days later on 21st August in Anson N9877 which came down in the sea off Nevin. My log book shows that I flew in three other Ansons which later were lost flying from Penrhos, N9551 on 2.9.41, N4884 on 24.10.41, and N9532 on 13.11.41.' This was like playing Russian Roulette for the crews.

By 1942 the training of observers was mainly undertaken by the Dominions under the Empire Air Training Scheme, the one exception being No.5 AOS at Jurby in the Isle of Man, left as a yardstick by which to measure overseas training. This left a need for units in the UK to hold month long courses for graduates to acclimatise themselves to

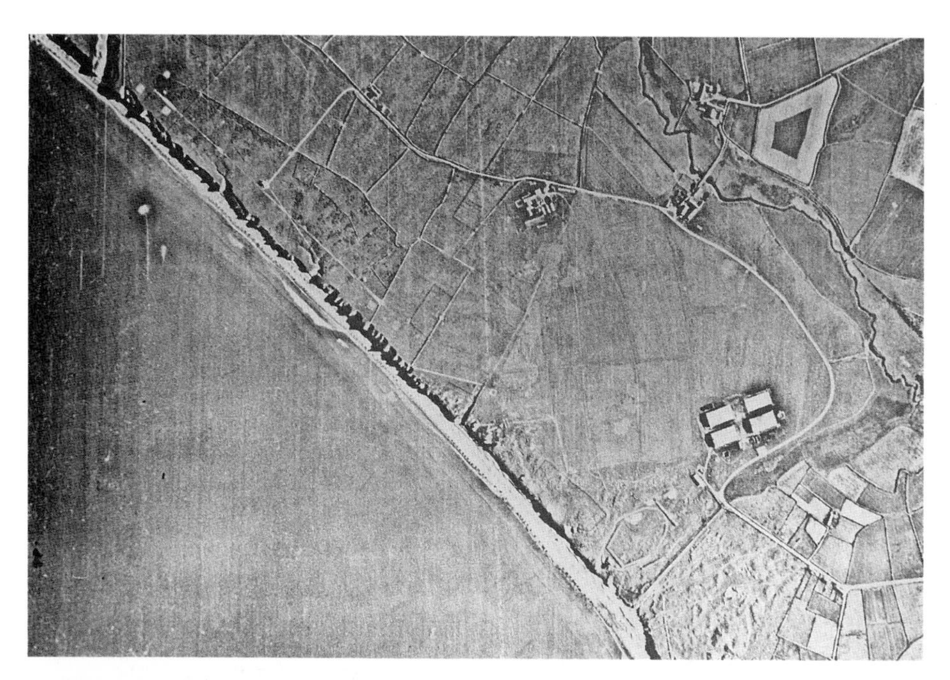

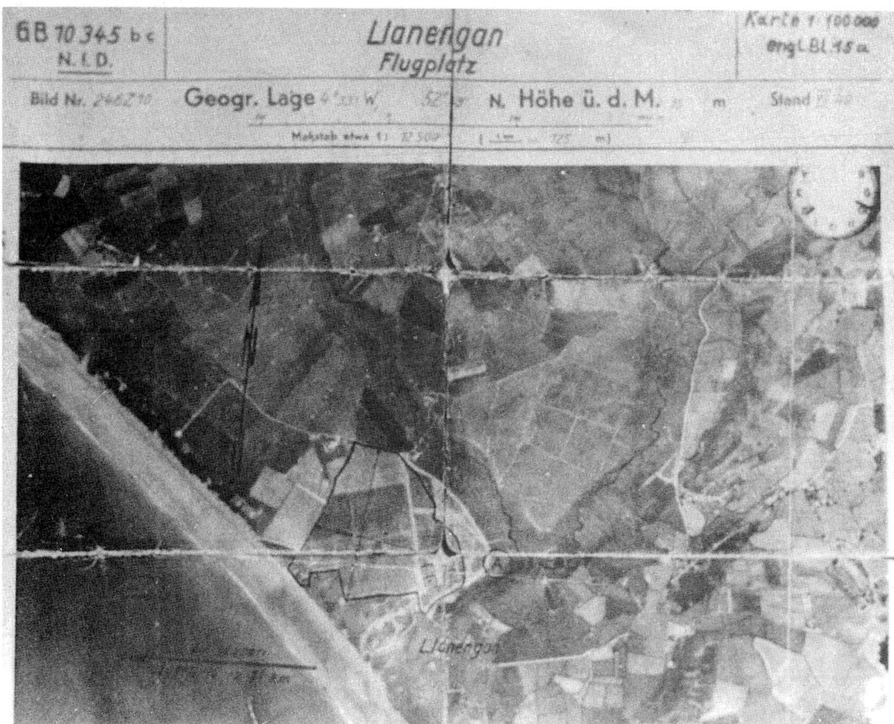
GB 10 345 bc
N. I. D.
Llanengan
Flugplatz
Karte 1: 100 000
engl. Bl. 15 a
Bild Nr.
Geogr. Lage
N.
Höhe ü. d. M.
m
Stand
Llanengan

Air gunners on the moving target range at Hell's Mouth. *Chaz Bowyer*

A formidable machine gun emplacement overlooking Hell's Mouth is one of the largest wartime remains.

Sergeant George Blagden, Penrhos staff pilot in 1938.

the crowded airspace, the few aids to navigation available, and the totally different weather. Most of the training time was spent in the air. Penrhos changed over to this system on 1st May 1942, as No.9 (Observers) Advanced Flying Unit, but with night flying being carried out from Llandwrog where a detachment of six Ansons operated. The vastly increased numbers of aircrew spilled over from the camp and were found accommodation in the nearby towns and villages, including Abersoch, Llanbedrog, and Pwllheli. On Saturday nights there was the usual mad rush to Pwllheli where the pubs, the White Hart for one (only open from 6 to 9pm) were full, followed with a visit to Margaret's chip shop, run by two sisters, then onto the dance hall, open until 11pm. On closing, those fortunate enough to be accompanied by a young lady would see her home. More often than not she lived in the opposite direction to Penrhos! As the buses had stopped running for the night, a stream of airmen could be seen staggering towards their temporary home. Those arriving after midnight would circumvent the guardhouse and dive through a convenient hole to be found in a ditch under the barbed wire, and thence to their huts to collapse on a bed. Sundays were not popular, with everywhere closed on the typical Welsh Sabbath of those days. With its better facilities, Llandwrog took over the control of No.9(O)AFU on 11th February 1943, so allowing Penrhos to concentrate on Air Gunners courses. The last of these, No.60, was completed on 25th November 1944. At the end of the war Penrhos briefly became an Aircrew Holding Unit, and closed down on 31st March 1946. A home for Polish ex-servicemen now covers part of the accommodation site, and a select caravan park occupies the area where hangars once stood, though a few wartime buildings survive. A small strip at the western edge of the airfield has since been used occasionally for light aircraft, mainly in the summer months.

RAF Hell's Mouth

Looking at the site of this former landing ground today, smaller even than Penrhos, it is difficult to visualise how the larger twin engined aircraft such as Blenheims and Whitleys managed to land here. There were certainly a few in the hangars. It opened at the same time as Penrhos with targets for air-gunnery practice situated on the sand dunes separating the beach from the airfield, and target floats in the bay itself for bombing practice. With the outbreak of war further facilities were required. The building of a moving target range for air gunners was started, which involved laying an oval narrow gauge rail track for a large plywood aircraft model propelled by an electric motor, and associated buildings, which was completed by July 1940. An extension to the landing ground was obviously needed and this, with new accommodation, was ready by the end of May 1941. The airfield was run by an officer, a few NCOs, and thirty groundstaff. With air gunners firing on the moving target range, and airborne gunners firing at the fixed targets on the cliff top near the moving target, Hell's Mouth was potentially a dangerous place to be. On one occasion there were three target checkers waiting behind a concrete wall to do their work. During a brief lull, one of them left the safety of the wall to run for milk for their tea break just a short distance away to the camp. An aircraft swept over the , targets, guns blazing, at that instant and he was killed.

Ted Lane was stationed here from November 1942 to September 1943 and recalls: 'Those of us operating the moving target range, an electrician and a couple of airmen to change models shredded by gunfire, were housed in a shelter on the seaward side of the track and in contact with the NCO in charge of the trainee gunners. No way did we show ourselves until we had the All Clear! Even some of the first Yank air gunners over here were sent to us to use the moving target range. They created chaos in our dining

Westland Wallace K8685 crash. Flight Lieutenant Walker and AC Lindsell were uninjured. Note target flag containers on lower sides of the fuselage. *George Blagden*

room about the basic rations we had endured for three years of war, but we found them a happy bunch. Hell's Mouth was predominantly a bombing range for trainee bomb aimers flying out of Penrhos. Two targets, consisting of rafts about twenty feet square, were moored about a mile off shore. They had a short mast surmounted by a basket type of ball for our benefit when sighting during a bomb drop. This was carried out from Quadrants, huts with large windows overlooking the bay, containing a bench on which was fixed a semi circular brass ring etched with compass bearings, and a telescope on a swivel. When an Anson made its bombing run the man sighting would watch the target and as soon as the smoke bomb erupted, he would sight onto it while his mate would take the bearing and telephone it to Penrhos where it was plotted. Each Anson would drop six eleven pound bombs, taking about twenty minutes in all. Three quadrants were built, No.1 at the eastern end of the cliffs, No.2 on cliffs near the airfield, and No.3 situated at the western end of the bay. This was my favourite, despite a long cycle ride, with wonderful views of Hell's Mouth bay and, in summer one could call at a local farm to purchase eggs or pick mushrooms to add to our menu. Night bombing was very occasional, and co operation arranged from No.2 Quadrant, the only one which had a searchlight. When we were informed of an Anson on its way we would switch the searchlight on and aim it at the moored target. No bearings were taken as this was just to give the bomb aimer an idea of night bombing. One night the pilot and bomb aimer lost their sense of direction and bombed the wrong end of the searchlight beam. A flash bomb burst close to the Quadrant entailing a frantic phone call to Penrhos!'

Though the landing ground was subject to sea mists, and closed at times, it was intended as a relief airfield for Penrhos and several aircraft including those of the USAAF, lost and short of fuel, found sanctuary here. One of the few crashes here took place on 3rd August 1944 when Wellington X3541 of No.18 OTU suffered an engine failure in the locality. The Polish pilot overshot during the forced belly landing and ended up hitting a concealed brick wall on the edge of a cornfield to the north east of the airfield, thankfully with no serious casualties.

A little known offshoot activity of this airfield was to provide personnel for the manning of a decoy 'Q' site on the headland to the east, above Porth Ceiriad. A set of lights, powered by a generator, to simulate a runway were switched on when enemy aircraft were in the area to convince the crews they were over Penrhos. This may not have been very popular with any locals who knew its purpose, but it was never bombed. It may even have been a useful navigation point for the enemy.

The noise of simulated battle died down in the summer of 1945, and that wild and beautiful foreshore resumed its former peaceful glory.

The pilot survived this Harrow crash just off Penrhos airfield on 8th September 1939.

Penrhos line up, 1939-40. Mk.I short nose Blenheims K7087 'F', nearest the camera, and 'H', plus Ansons coded '10' and '4'.
Both George Blagden

Chapter Two

RAF Llandwrog

The name of this airfield was taken from a nearby stone built village, which in turn derives its name from the cell, or church, of Saint Twrog, a sixth century Welsh missionary. Indeed, the airfield, now Caernarfon Airport, is situated on an historic peninsula. To the north lies the Napoleonic Fort Belan, guarding the western entrance to the Menai Strait, while to the south stands Dinas Dinlle, an Iron Age fortification, with a later Roman fortress. Incongruously, a Second World War 'seagull' machine gun post in the lower slopes faces the airfield it was intended to guard. A short distance away, the Roman Watling Street is said to have terminated here. At the airfield, pleasure flights include trips around Snowdon. Fifty years ago such excursions were to be avoided at all costs. The reasons will be found in the following pages.

As the German Army steamrollered through France in the early summer of 1940 it became apparent to the Air Ministry that their worst fears would soon be realised. Not only would the RAF soon be fighting for our immediate survival, but we would be open to attack from the west within a matter of weeks. So it was then that Air Commodore Darley and his surveyors arrived on the Morfa Dinlle peninsula south of Caernarvon while searching for sites for fighter airfields in the northwest. He soon completed a survey for the site and construction work began in September, the contract having been awarded to Sir Alfred McAlpine's company, with sub contracts going to British Runways Ltd, and local firms. However, with the lessening of enemy air activity due to the move to the Russian front of many Luftwaffe squadrons at the end of May 1941, the need for more fighter stations diminished. There was though a continuing threat of some enemy activity in the Midlands, and north west, and the need for a training airfield out of the main line of fire was soon felt. Airspeed Oxfords of No.11 SFTS were flown in from Shawbury on 11th June 1941 for night flying practice from the new tarmac runways before an official opening. The first fatal accident here took place on the 24th June when Oxford T3933 stalled on take off and dived into the sea, with the loss of the trainee pilot, Cadet Bobbie Daly, of Belfast, who was the first airman interred in the CWGC plot at Llanbeblig Cemetery, Caernarvon.

RAF Llandwrog officially opened as No.9 Air Gunners School on 7th July 1941, as part of 25 Group, Flying Training Command. On the 16th, a Polish pilot of No.2 Ferry Pilots Pool, was bringing in Whitley T4153 when he made a poor approach and opened up the engines to go round again. He was unable to climb away, and hit a building, skidded on the ground, did a spectacular nose up, then demolished another building, and survived. The training was soon well under way through the long summer hours, but the 10th October brought a terrible tragedy. Whitleys K7252 and K9041 collided onto the runway while in the process of landing with the loss of all seventeen airmen on board. This was the main aircraft type for pupil air gunners to train in, though there were some single engined Boulton Paul Defiants, a type which had a dorsal gun turret fitted. Westland Lysanders performed the task of towing the target drogues. The AGS stayed until 13th June 1942, when it closed, though some air gunner and bombing training was carried out

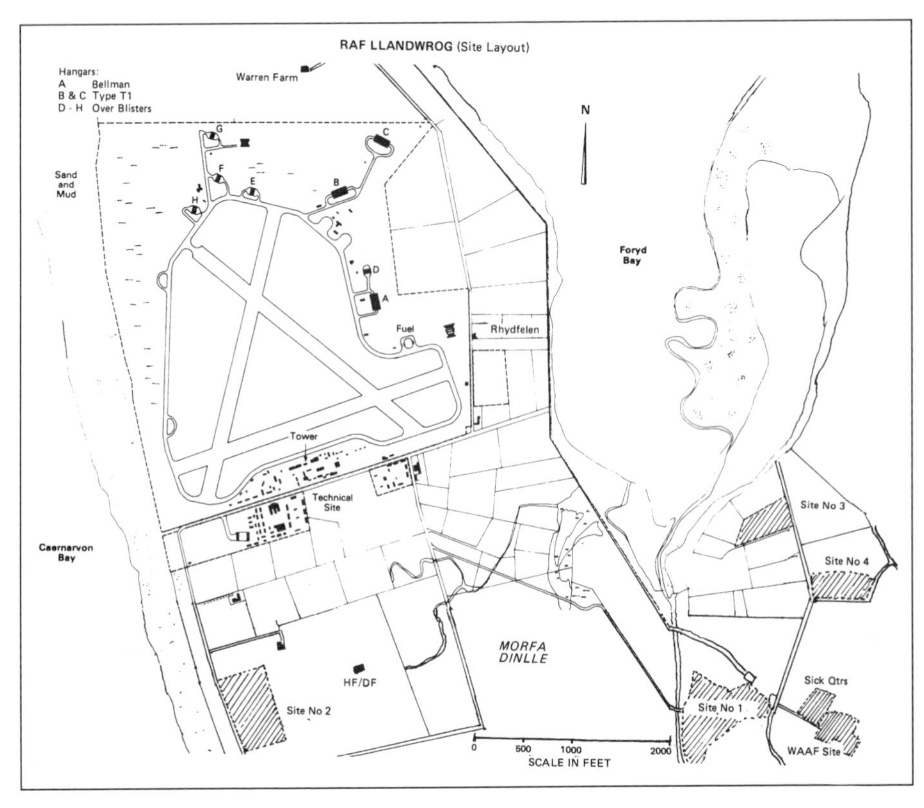

from Penrhos. The station then extended its activities with No.9 (Observers) Advanced Flying Unit, still headquartered at Penrhos. The night flying Ansons increased several-fold off the flarepath tarmac runways, against the six operating the night shift since January.

The various accommodation sites were sensibly scattered away from the airfield with its technical site, but No.2 site was built on low lying land opposite the beach and the occupants of the huts suffered cold water-logged huts often in the winter months. In these circumstances keeping the cast iron stove alight in the centre of each hut was of prime importance. Not all the excitement was in the air. Noel Bailey was a flight mechanic at Llandwrog for most of the war years: 'It was the duty of the earliest riser to tend to the stove, Ginger and Taffy were nearest to it. On this particular morning it had gone out and Taffy decided to get it going with the help of a can of petrol kept under his bed. He poured petrol onto damp wood and paper which hadn't taken, then lit a match at the opening. With a great roar a sheet of flame shot between Taffy's legs. He was wearing only a shirt and it singed all the hair off his legs, and higher. The stove top blew off and landed on Ginger's head as he sat up, almost braining him. The explosion filled the hut with acrid smoke and burnt paper. To those awakened by the bang it seemed as if they had been hit by a bomb.

Ginger attracted ill luck. One night Ansons were recalled due to bad weather moving in. A searchlight was beamed vertically as an aid to the returning crews. Ginger, who like many, never had enough cash for a battery for his cycle lamp, was on the far side of the airfield. Using the bonus of the light from the

RAF Llandwrog vertical in May 1946.
RAF photograph, Crown copyright

Llandwrog camp water tower in 1978, since demolished.

Camp buildings near main entrance.

Air Sea Rescue launch crew at Fort Belan.
Wally Norman via Bob Roberts

searchlight he started off cycling round the perimeter track. As he reached a critical bend, the light was suddenly extinguished and he went straight on into a trench filled with water. He appeared at the hut door much later with the bicycle wrapped round his neck and squelching like a half drowned rat.'

Airfield defence was provided by anti-aircraft positions, and machine gun posts situated at strategic places. The beach, above the high water mark, was heavily mined to prevent a seaborne attack. During the removal of these late in the war, a bomb disposal officer was killed. The only enemy attack however came on 23rd January 1942 when all Llandwrog aircraft were grounded due to bad weather. A lone Junkers Ju 88 roared in at fifty feet, machine-gunned targets of opportunity, and vanished just as swiftly. The local postman dived into a ditch and never had to buy a drink in the pub for years as he recounted the adventure to anyone who would listen. Only one Whitley, P5024, was slightly damaged but the attack livened up a dull day. The Junkers may have been from 3/Kustenfliegergruppe 106 which lost several aircraft around this time on coastal reconnaissance and mine-laying duties.

Rescue facilities were handled by two high speed launches of the RAF No.63 Air Sea Rescue Unit based at Fort Belan, a Napoleonic fort with a dock, built on the tip of the peninsula. The crews were constantly at sea searching for airmen of ditched aircraft from the many coastal airfields in the northwest.

The airfield itself was a busy place with many aircraft movements each day and night. Inevitably accidents were commonplace. On 15th May 1943 Wellington BK139 from No.30 OTU at Hixon in Staffordshire, was on a night flight in the area when the port engine began to emit smoke and sparks, then cut out. The instructor took over from the pupil pilot and made an emergency landing. In doing so he made too tight a circuit, lost height, and crashed on the airfield. The Wellington caught fire and ammunition started exploding. The ground staff on duty immediately raced over, even though it was not known if the aircraft carried bombs. The

RAF rescue pinnace, built at Pwllheli and based at Menai Bridge in 1942. Maximum speed was 14 knots with three Parkinson diesel engines. *Wally Norman via Bob Roberts*

Llandwrog flying control tower, photographed in 1978.

Oxford R6329 of 11 SFTS from Shawbury, which undershot at Llandwrog on 10th July 1941. *Tom Yates*

Ex-Llandwrog east-west runway faces into the mountains.

pilot extricated himself, but the six remaining crew were all in the wreckage in a dazed and injured state. Without waiting for the fire tender to get into full operation and protect them with foam, Sergeant R.A.C.Grimshaw, and Corporal A.E.Mills, along with three other Airmen, crawled into the burning wreckage and brought five crew members out. Reg Martin, of the MR Team, found the rear gunner caught fast in his turret by his hair, so proceeded to give him a hasty Mohican haircut and assist the gunner out. When the air gunner first saw the result in a mirror, he threatened to have Martin court-martialled!

As the NCOs leading the rescue, Sergeant Grimshaw and Corporal Mills were later awarded the BEM (Military) for displaying a complete disregard for their own safety in effecting this rescue. All the injured were taken to the naval hospital, HMS Glendower (later Butlins Holiday Camp) near Pwllheli, but one died later. The investigation showed that the engine problem was due to failure of the sleeve and piston assembly of one cylinder.

Summer months found cadets from the Air Training Corps squadrons in the general area taking odd day visits or week long camps here. As a training station there was a much better chance of being taken for flights than at operational units. RAF Llandwrog then was a highly prized objective with long navigational flights in the AFU Ansons possible. Ken Davies, of No.1394 (Llandudno Town) Squadron, joined the ATC in May 1942. One week later, even before he had been issued with a uniform, he went on a day visit to Llandwrog. A Polish pilot took him up in one of the Lysanders and treated him to a hair-raising flight under the Menai Suspension Bridge. Not all the flights were so agreeable.

On the 28th August 1943 twenty two cadets and one officer from No.271 (Colwyn Bay) and No.418 (Aberconway) Squadrons arrived for the week. They were due to leave on the morning of Saturday 4th September, but their transport was delayed. Cadets Geoffrey Foulkes and Geoffrey Stapleton managed to obtain a flight on Anson EG278 for a short night flying test with the pilot and staff wireless operator. Arthur Jones was a cadet from a Blaenau Ffestiniog squadron, spending a few days with a friend in Caernarvon. 'We were on our bikes watching the approach of an Anson from Llandwrog. It passed over us at a height of about 1,500 feet and was heading for Caernarvon station when suddenly most of the port wing fell off and came down like a falling leaf. The Anson flipped over and fell towards the Menai Strait. We got on our bikes and headed through town onto the Bangor road where a police car overtook us. Just off the main road at Parciau Farm we saw the true extent of the disaster. The Anson had crashed upside down, ploughed through a hedge, and come to rest in the middle of a field. The Police and ARP prevented us from going too close but we could see four bodies and a partly opened parachute. The next day we had a visit from Flight Lieutenant Faulkner who was investigating the accident. It was only then that we found out that two cadets had been on board.'

The writer was in the ATC Guard of Honour at the service for the two cadets held later at Llandrillo-yn-Rhos Church, followed by the military funeral for Cadet Foulkes. Cadet Stapleton had been evacuated to North Wales to escape the perils of the Blitz, and his body was taken to East Ham for burial. Nearly fifty years on that emotional experience would be the trigger for the writer to compile a Roll of Honour for all cadets who lost their lives while serving with the Corps for the 50th Anniversary of the ATC. The Anson pilot, Pilot Officer L.A.Walker is buried in Llanbeblig Cemetery, Caernarvon, along with many airmen from Snowdonia's crashes. He had previously survived a ditching in Anson DJ627 on 15th May 1943, after an engine had blown up while flying off Anglesey.

Ronald S.Sledge, a staff pilot here from October 1942 to January 1944, and later a pilot with BOAC, recalls 'I made three landings away from base due to engine failure. Also on 29th January and 30th April 1943 I flew Ansons on airsea rescue duties in an effort to locate ditched aircraft of the USAAF. On another occasion a Douglas Boston made a forced landing and overran the runway into the sandhills where its nosewheel was on the edge of the minefield. It was recovered very gingerly! The rest of the time I flew day and night shepherding U/T (under training) navigators around the sky for flights lasting around three hours. The monotony was only broken by an air test affording the opportunity to 'beat up' the area round the Great Orme and, on one occasion, to inspect the underside of the Menai Bridge. I also have fond recollections of the Castle Inn in Caernarvon, where the first pint was always on the house, and I believe the Landlord's daughter married an Australian pilot from Llandwrog.' Another favourite watering hole was The Harp (Ty Llan, called the Tin Can), in Llandwrog village, run by Geraint and Ann Griffith. This was in particular a haunt of Australian airmen, and one night the singing became so boisterous that the floor gave way and the occupants fell through to the cellar! Many staff pilots started off their North Wales experience by being posted to Penrhos and then moved on to Llandwrog to only take on night flying after becoming familiar with the area. Hubert Scrivener was one, and recalls loading up the Anson with his motor bike and a barrel of beer for the transfer.

The flying continued apace throughout the war to prepare aircrew for their eventual roles. One of the problems raising its head here was airsickness. Those airmen who had trained in calmer climes were now subjected at times to much worse weather over the Irish Sea and buffeting over the mountains. Many had travelled to the UK on long sea voyages, and had lost their 'air' legs after not flying for months. Some were so ill they could not carry on their tasks, and had to be taken off courses, with all that training wasted.

The largest aircraft to land here was an operational Lancaster in the summer of 1943, flown in by a former staff pilot to show his chums what they could aspire to if they survived the training flights.

The contribution from the WAAF contingent here was considerable, serving in the Sick Bay, parachute section, administration, as cooks, in transport, and meteorology, to name a few. In addition to these duties, their presence was an immense boost to morale. The senior WAAF towards the end of hostilities was Section Officer Joan Roman, wife of General Roman, head of the Free Belgian Forces.

On 14th June 1945 the Advanced Flying Unit was disbanded, and No.2 Aircrew Holding Unit moved in for a while, processing many Canadians for release, until its job was done. From September 1946 until 1955

No.277 MU occupied the airfield and had the dangerous task, codename 'Operation Sandcastle', of storing 9,000 tons of German Army chemical warfare weapons. This was housed in eight hangars erected on the northeast/southwest runway. The local schoolchildren were instructed to keep their gas masks long after those in the rest of Britain, the potential hazard being so lethal. The gas was removed in 1955 and taken via Fort Belan out to the SS *Empire Clair* which was later scuttled off Rockall in the Atlantic. In 1969 the airfield was given a new lease of life when the east-west runway was resurfaced for use by aircraft in the run up to, and during the Investiture of the Prince of Wales at Caernarfon, and used since for civil flying. In 1989 an Air Museum was opened on the airfield and includes an interesting exhibition of photographs of the RAF Llandwrog Mountain Rescue Team, and much else. This is an opportune place to remind ourselves that airmen were all volunteers. As they made that commitment, they would not have dreamed that the hazards of mountain and sea came into the realms of preparing for battle in the air.

The following chapters will hopefully give a little insight into life at RAF Llandwrog from the point of view of airmen, both staff and trainees, who flew from there. It is then a natural progression into Part II to discover how the birth of the Llandwrog RAF Mountain Rescue Team came about, so closely associated with many of the station's aircraft and crews.

Geoffrey Foulkes, aged 8, later to lose his life in Anson EG278 flying from Llandwrog.
Ken Stott

Cadets of No.1394 (Llandudno Town) Air Training Corps Squadron, awaiting Anson flights, on Llandwrog airfield in July 1943.
Ken Davies (third from left)

Chapter Three

Air Gunnery Days

On 7th July 1941 No.9 Air Gunners School was formed at Llandwrog from personnel and aircraft formerly operating No.9 Bombing and Gunnery School at Penrhos. The aircraft were some twelve ancient (by aviation standards) Whitley bombers, cast off by operational squadrons and Operational Training Units. The early Marks had manually operated gun turrets which were awkward to manage, but Marks IV and V had powered turrets. There were innumerable hold ups: no intercom, engine and other failures, the Lysander used for target towing not turning up, and the terrible weather in winter which closed flying down and put the courses back. Also in use were some Defiant single engined fighters which had a dorsal gun turret. The Whitleys would fly sedately over Caernarvon Bay, while the trainee air gunners in the front and rear turrets would endeavour to hit the drogues towed by the Lysanders, flying on the seaward side of them for obvious reasons.

Part of their training included visits to the moving target range at Hell's Mouth. Here a large model aircraft travelled at speed on a trolley running on an oval railway track, and the gunners practised firing at this from a portable gun turret. Everyone else kept their heads down! Penrhos was also visited twice weekly to practise on a panoramic turret in one of the hangars.

Les Sidwell was at Llandwrog on No.8 Air Gunners Course from January to March 1942 and recalls: 'I have happy memories of Llandwrog and they are not wiped out by the atrocious weather in that wild spot. It was a time of tearing gales, icy cold with snow and sleet. Heavy rain with resultant floods on the camp. There was much snow round the outside area, cutting off the camp for days with no mail or papers. There were some remarkable changes; a nice mild sunny day would abruptly change after tea, back to the roaring gales all night and through the next day. Flying was badly upset and we spent much time hanging around the crew room in hopes of better forecasts. Every night the din of the angry sea grinding away on the pebbles and the bitter cold (despite piling everything possible on the beds) kept us awake. The roofs leaked so badly that the floors were swimming with water. You hoped not to have to go outside to have a pee in the floods outside in the icy gales. Our planned trips to Penrhos or Hell's Mouth to use their training facilities were mostly aborted due to the weather and our old buses breaking down. We had some fun in the midst of all this. One morning we got as far as Llanaelhearn where five lorries were stuck in deep snow. We had to manhandle our old crock round to return to Llandwrog which was snow free. We only made it once to Hell's Mouth to use the moving target range. When we did start to catch up with some flying it was to be faced \with an emergency situation.

On 25th January I was one of six pupil air gunners in Whitley N1475 with pilot Flying Officer Allan Watson. We were carrying out an air-to-air exercise stooging along parallel to the coast. Suddenly the port engine cut dead and the pilot at once turned to port for the nearest land as we lost height. I was with the pilot whilst all this went on and, since there was no intercom, was deputed to crawl through the narrow 'tunnel' in the wing spar to warn the others to brace themselves for a crash landing. Also to get the cockpit door open for a quick exit in case of fire. After this I crawled back to the cockpit in time to see us making a landfall approach, losing height on the one engine, near the golf links at the headland near Morfa Nevin. As the other engine cut I saw how skilfully the pilot handled the old Whitley as the sea beneath us vanished and we were whizzing along over some grass to crunch with the undercarriage up and judder violently along the bumpy surface. No fire broke out and we all survived. There was one casualty; one pupil had been poorly since take off and had dozed off in the fuselage. When he was roused for the emergency he didn't follow what was going on as the door was opened. He came to as we skidded along the green turf. Thinking it was the sea, and that he had to jump into the 'water' to survive, he jumped out. Fortunately this was just before the aircraft came to a stop, and all he suffered from was a sprained ankle. We crossed the field to the Linksway Hotel where the proprietors treated us like VIPs with a lovely Sunday dinner and drinks.'

In the spring of 1942 the AGS was called upon to provide three Whitley bombers (N1345, N1428, and T1455) along with their pilots and wireless operator/air gunner instructors to bolster numbers to the magic figure of 1,000 aircraft for the largest aerial bombardment to date, on Cologne which took place on the night of 30/31 May. On the way back to their temporary base at Driffield, Whitley N1345 was shot down. Sergeant W.H.Orman went down with it, trapped in the rear turret. As the aircraft broke up, Pilot Officer Dennis Box, a New Zealander, passed a parachute to the pilot, Squadron Leader John Russell, who managed to clip it on as he fell through space, and survived, but the donor was unable to save himself. The other two crews and their Whitleys returned safely to Llandwrog a few days later, but the two crew who had flown in N1428 died in 1943. Pilot Officer Jack Croudis, RNZAF, died on 1st March with his crew of four when Anson EJ129 crashed on the banks of the River Llyfni following an obscure engine failure at night. The wireless operator/air gunner, Sergeant A.J.Harvey was killed on 15th March when Blenheim V6127 was in collision with Blenheim R3908 during take off at Penrhos.

Later, following the closure of the Air Gunners School in June 1942, some air gunnery training was transferred to Penrhos where it continued its vital work.

Armstrong Whitworth Whitley, a type extensively used at the Air Gunnery School. *Chaz Bowyer*

Westland Lysanders, L4791 nearest the camera. A type used extensively as a target tower by No.9AGS. *Westland Aircraft*

Pilot Officer Les Sidwell, promoted off his air gunners course in February 1941

Chapter Four

Perils of a Staff Pilot

By the time Llandwrog settled into the role as parent of No.9(O)AFU, there were a large number of Ansons Mk.I on the airfield, some sixty for the same number of navigators in each intake, plus a reserve for maintenance and losses. This in turn required a similar number of staff pilots to fly them. They came from two backgrounds; most from pilots advanced flying units (P)AFUs, where they had progressed through flying training to handle twin engined aircraft, and many via a Staff Pilot Training Unit at Cark, on Morecambe Bay. Also, as the war progressed, a few experienced pilots came here after surviving an operational tour, for a rest!

The Commanding Officer (Flying) was Squadron Leader Brackenbury, with Flight Lieutenant Faulkner his second in command, whose duty it was to vet new pilots and, where necessary, convert them onto the Anson, and carry out periodic checks of competence in beam approach used at night or bad weather. Their flying skills would also be checked periodically in the 'Link' trainer, a flight simulator. The Adjutant late in the war was Cledwyn Hughes who, after the war, became a local Member of Parliament and was later elevated to the Peerage.

A staff pilot would have a staff wireless operator on board and often form a regular team, building up confidence in each other's abilities. They were organised into one of four flights, AI & AII, BI & BII. The A flights would take the daylight stint for a fortnight, while B flight carried out the night flying. The two groups would then change over. All this required the associated ground crews to fuel and maintain the aircraft. Thus the airfield was operating 24 hours a day.

There were usually two navigational day or two night trips. Each aircraft detailed for night flying was checked out by a pilot and wireless operator in daytime with a 20 minute flight, a Night Flying Test (NFT). In poor weather conditions the crews took the 'Milk Run', Base-Fishguard-Chicken Rock (Isle of Man)-Base. The staff pilot was not just a chauffeur to his crews. He had to fly accurately by day and night, both visually, and by instruments in all weathers. He had to keep a mental track of the courses they were on and advise the navigator, where necessary and prudent, for the safety of the aircraft. The composition of crews would vary. At times, with only navigation courses being run, there would be two or three under training (U/T) navigators flying with the pilot and staff wireless operator. At other times there would be a nucleus bomber crew on board, staff pilot, with a trainee navigator, bomb aimer, and wireless operator. The last three would go on to an operational training unit, where complete bomber crews would be made up with a regular pilot, a flight engineer, and air gunners. Maurice Bryan was OC No.A2 Flight Ansons: 'Llandwrog was a dangerous little airfield. It stood on a peninsula with the sea on three sides. On the landward side was the Snowdonia mountain range. It is undoubtedly attractive and beloved by residents, tourists, and climbers alike. To us however it posed a dangerous and forbidding threat. As we approached the airfield from the sea the mountains lay ahead and we had a safety height of 3,500 feet. We were always aware that one mistake, one error of judgement, would put us amongst those mountains and, sadly, it happened too many times to allow any of us to become complacent. If our efforts were unheroic they were far from

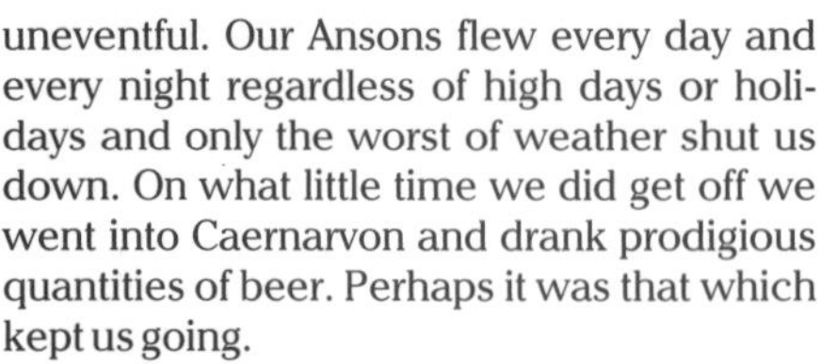

Staff pilot Ron Sledge. *Hope Roberts*

Staff pilots Maurice Bryan left, with his fiancee, and Jack Stephenson, with his wife, by the swing bridge near Caernarfon Castle.

uneventful. Our Ansons flew every day and every night regardless of high days or holidays and only the worst of weather shut us down. On what little time we did get off we went into Caernarvon and drank prodigious quantities of beer. Perhaps it was that which kept us going.

My own near disaster at Llandwrog came not from the sea, nor the mountains, but from above. I was up one night miles over the sea. It was a dirty night full of yellow cloud and storm. Suddenly, without warning of what was to come, we were struck by lightning. It hit the trailing aerial and ran up and blew a great hole in the side of the aircraft. A howling wind frightened the life out of us. The enormous electrical charge magnetised the airframe and all the instruments went haywire. We were without radio or compasses. I turned through what I hoped was 180 degrees and headed for home. After what seemed to be an eternity I saw the coast of Anglesey come up and shortly afterwards the Menai Strait which I followed home. We had made it, but it was an experience I wouldn't care to repeat'.

There were also incidents on the airfield itself stemming from flying old, hardused aircraft. Bryan again: 'As one of four Flight Commanders I had to take my share as officer in charge of night flying. This meant spending the night in Flying Control and generally directing events. My friend Jack Stephenson was flying one night and, as he was approaching the airfield, he radioed to say that he couldn't get his undercarriage down. He circled the field and tried everything he knew to get the wheels down, and we gave what advice we could from the tower. All the time there were other aircraft coming home and stacked up, waiting to land. Clearly we had to do something. Stephenson was instructed to bring his Anson in 'belly-up' on the grass alongside the runway. This he managed to do with considerable skill, as the rest of us held our breath, and without anyone getting hurt. To spell it out in words is to do no justice to what was a remarkable piece of night flying'.

Ray Chadbourne arrived after operational service with several night fighter squadrons, the last being 288 Squadron. He recalls 'Because of my night vision, I was one of the pilots nominated as a pathfinder, and we used to take off about half an hour before everyone else. If the trip was to Scotland we used to go ahead and, if the weather was bad, radio to base and this would save the main force from taking off and having to be recalled. Weather forecasting was very limited at the time, so our contribution was invaluable. Bad weather over Snowdonia was dicey. My scheme was to come back to base by radio beam at a safe height, then fly due west so that I was over the sea, then come down almost to sea level, approach the coast and, recognising the local landmarks, make for the airfield and land'.

Of the pilots arriving for their first posting, the first few weeks were the most hazardous until they became familiar with the area. Many of the crashes happened to the inexperienced. Arthur Bickerdike arrived on 22nd July 1943. On 23rd August he was returning in cloud to Llandwrog in Anson N5371, from a flight to Shrewsbury, following a course given by a trainee navigator. Suddenly he saw sheep on a mountainside just beneath him and managed to stall onto the slope just under the summit of 3,091 feet Foel Fras. Fortunately all the five crew survived with only bruises and were rescued later in the day by the Llandwrog MR Unit.

George Bates arrived at Llandwrog during its most tragic days, on 1st June 1942: 'The really important factor was to get a good staff pilot staff wireless operator combination. The developed cooperation between these two was essential to survival. Often the trainee navigators would get lost due to lack of aids, bad weather etc. Then survival depended on the staff crew and, of course, LUCK! I eventually established a great combination with Sergeant Ken Coward as my W/OP. We were both newly married and lived off the base, so had much in common. The more you flew, the safer it became, because you got more skilful and canny in handling the terrain and the weather. Let me tell you of the night Ken Archer crashed. We were on route from Shrewsbury to Rhyl before a turn along the coast to base. On the leg to Rhyl I asked the navigator where he thought we were, and he seemed quite confident that we were on track. However, I still felt quite uneasy and suddenly, I don't know why, I told the navigator I was altering course

Staff pilot Ray Chadbourne. *Hope Roberts*

Staff pilot George Bates, who retired as a Wing Commander in 1968.

60 degrees to starboard. He was not happy, but I had this hunch and stuck to it. We came out of cloud on this new course and saw Rhyl dead ahead! Subsequently we plotted our original course and track on the given wind and found our position was directly on route to Carnedd Llewelyn and below its height. We had been two minutes behind Ken Archer's aircraft which crashed about a mile from that mountain.

Even such grim times can have a humourous side. Sergeant Davis, a South African wireless operator in the RAF, crashed twice on take off at night. The first time they went down soon after take off and thought they were landing on the sands. Davis opened the aircraft door and jumped out, and landed in deep water. The Coastguard at the nearest point suddenly had a group of bedraggled and wet figures come up the

Staff pilot Keith Shalless, RAAF.

Sergeant Arthur Bickerdike and crew survived the crash of Anson N5371 on the summit of Foel Fras on 28th July 1943.
A Bickerdike

Staff pilots in April 1945, just before closure of 9 (O) AFU. Middle row, Squadron Leader Faulkner centre, CO Flying, flanked by Flight Commanders including Flying Officer Rhude 4th left. *David T Searle, 3rd left, back row*

beach. Six months later Davis was in another aircraft that crashed on take off. Davis, not to be fooled by the tide this time, opened the door and threw the dinghy out. Only this time the tide was out and the dinghy bounced up in the air! The crew, dry and safe, walked up the beach again.

Days off were fun, the Caernarvon pubs, The Anglesey, Hole in the Wall, The Royal Hotel, we enjoyed them all, and the dances at the Drill Hall. So many romances and marriages to local girls eventuated. I met Gladys Mary Jones, in a taxi on the way to a dance at the Sergeant's Mess. I took her home and proposed to her that very night! We married three months later at the church in Castle Square, and we had a four day honeymoon in Rhyl.' George Bates survived a tour in Bomber Command and stayed in the RAF until 1968, retiring as a Wing Commander and emigrating to New Zealand, where he kept on flying.

One of the last staff pilots to arrive in October 1944 was Keith Shalless RAAF, from Victoria, who stayed until late April 1945. 'I still recall vividly a 4 hour night trip over 10/10ths cloud all the way. We started on a northeast heading, then due south, and the last and longest leg westward. During all that time we never saw ground, the trainee wireless operator did not get even one accurate bearing because of stormy conditions, and the trainee navigator could only plot theoretical tracks and estimated time of arrival. The bomb aimer, who would normally be map reading and so helping to fix our position, was only useful in winding the undercarriage up and down. The trainees were suitably impressed when I suddenly made a major alteration of course and came down through cloud (not usually recommended), over Caernarvon Bay and exactly level with Llandwrog. As the Staff Pilot Course at Cark had taught me I had been doing my own mental DR (dead reckoning) and when I saw a bubble of cloud protruding through the other layer cloud I decided it just had to be from the upper slopes of Mount Snowdon. That was one of the few times I blessed that dangerous monster.

'Towards the end of my stay in the area the RAF higher command stretched our self survival to the limit. They removed the Pundit and Occult beacons, the latter on the 'drome itself flashing two Morse code letters in red. We were then instructed to fly to the navigator's pinpoint on his ETA, wherever that was, even at night, and this would give him his margin of error, or perhaps a resting place in Snowdonia!

'Better memories prevailed at times. A fall of snow overnight covered the whole area in a white and silent blanket. I was first off that day and, on our downwind leg, we saw our three wheel marks etched blackly in the snow, then only two as the tail wheel came up, then the unbroken snow at the instant of

lift off. A spectacular picture in black and white that temporarily silenced some outgoing young airmen.

'By that time there were only a few other Australian pilots left at Llandwrog, including Vic Young. There were often rude remarks about the crazy Aussies on such radio programmes as 'Much Binding in the Marsh'. However, Vic earned his flying pay one night when, just after take off and at very low level, something was sucked into an engine which then caught fire. The pilot had to make a very low level circuit mainly over water. An Anson's one engine performance was to say at the least abysmal. Adding to the excitement, the staff wireless operator tried to pull his trainee away from the radio so that he could send an emergency distress signal. In the process they became entangled in each other's plugs and cords. They were still trying to sort it all out when some fine flying resulted in a safe landing. Had they come down in the sea the result would have been very different.

'There was always a little humour to balance the trying times. One of the near casualties to an aircraft and crew occurred when a twenty feet deep ground mist slid in and the ground mortar fired the usual star burst to tell aircraft to stay in the air. Those on the ground watched, fascinated, as it nearly removed the tail of an Anson doing a low level exploratory pass. It was very undignified being shot at by your own side!

'One night crews were packed into the briefing hut listening to a pretty WAAF Meteorological Officer giving a confident weather forecast of clear skies and no rain. They departed into a steady drizzle and lowering cloud. The little WAAF running for shelter dropped her Met charts into a puddle. A sardonic voice from the darkness said "First time you've ever had rain on your bloody chart luv?".'

Staff pilots and wireless operators in 1943. Sgt. H. Scrivener, 2nd left. *Capt. R.S. Sledge*

Staff pilot Ray Robinson, RAAF, 2nd from left. *Evan L. Jones*

Chapter Five

Navigator Training

By the summer of 1942, the title Observer, originally earned by those who were trained in navigation and bomb-aiming, was discontinued (except for those already qualified) in favour of Navigator. This was used on its own for those employed in heavy bombers, which contained their own bomb-aimers, but with a suffix of (B) for those additionally trained in bombaiming in light/medium day bombers, (W) for those additionally trained as W/T operators i.e. for intruders, and (R) for those who specialised in AI radar for night fighters.

With much of the training carried out overseas, especially in Canada, it became essential to run courses in the UK for newly qualified navigators. This was to acclimatise airmen to the crowded airspace in Britain, along with inclement weather, with complete wartime blackout, and introduce them to some of the navigational aids and beacons available. The courses generally ran for four weeks and the training time was spent mostly in the air. Since these units were originally called Observers Advanced Flying Units (O)AFU's, the title stuck until the end of the war. In the Anson the navigator's position was situated immediately behind the pilot for ease of communication, should the intercom be unserviceable, or to pass maps and courses. It had a small table for charts, and a set of repeater instruments including air speed, altimeter, and compass. The navigator would give the pilot a course to fly for each leg of a journey, along with a safe height to keep to.

Len Lambert was one of the smaller numbers who completed his Elementary Air Navigation School course in Britain, at Bridgnorth, entirely theoretical. 'On arrival at Llandwrog it was a relief to get back in a real aircraft. Initially there was much map reading, coupled with oblique photography to prove we had been where we were supposed to. My first flight as first navigator was on 13th February 1943 to carry out a square search south of the Isle of Man for a missing aircraft. The search was unsuccessful. Then followed a series of day cross country flights, alternating as first or second navigator. The first carried out dead reckoning navigation, calculating and plotting courses, wind direction and velocities, while the second took bearings (astro shots). Additionally he wound the Anson undercarriage up and down. The flights became night exercises, including simulated bombing attacks on British towns and cities using an infra-red target marker. This recorded on the aircraft's camera, but were not visible to the crew. The average flight was between 2-3 hours. Being based at Llandwrog, with the sea at one side, and the mountains the other, concentrated the mind wonderfully'.

Having successfully navigated an aircraft back to its base one could at last sit back and wait for the pilot to bring the crew back safely onto the runway, and a hot meal in the Mess. It was not that simple for some. Bill Benton had carried out his navigator training at No.45 Air School, Oudtshoorn, Cape Province, in South Africa. Here was his first near death encounter in an Anson, which suddenly dived earthwards on an authorised low level flight at 250 feet over the scrubland of the Karoo. The South African pilot managed to pull out of the dive but, because of severe vibration, had to land at the nearest emergency strip. On disembarking from the aircraft they were asked by a member of the ground staff 'Did you catch the rabbit?' The

Llandwrog Navigation Course 248, August 1944. At least four of these airmen would lose their lives later on operations including Sergeant Bill Berry, middle row 2nd left. He was shot down by a German intruder on the night of 3/4th March 1945. He and his crew lost their lives as some 200 enemy fighters followed our bombers back to their bases and shot down twenty. The others were Sergeants Isterling, centre middle row, Reardon middle row 2nd right, and Knight front row 2nd right.
Ken Stott (front row 4th from right).

Interior of Anson Mk.1 with dual controls of Duxford IWM collection. The navigator's table is on the left, with boxes for sextant and charts. Above are repeater main instruments including altimeter and compass.
Author, by kind permission IWM Duxford

reason for this was that the tips of both propellers were turned up like the front of skis. They had been inches from extinction.

Bill Benton arrived at Llandwrog in August 1943 for the advanced flying course. This he completed with sufficient hours, but some course members had not achieved enough. Therefore on 27th August the whole course was detailed for a night flight. 'By tea time the weather had become quite bad with much cloud and rain. I was, with some of the others, having tea in Caernarvon and debating whether to return to camp early or not, expecting the flying to be scrubbed. We decided to go back, only to find that the flying was 'on', and we took off around midnight. We used the bad weather route called the 'Milk Run', and were approaching Cardigan, when we received, not unexpectedly, a recall. I had previously been recalled from an identical position and, in consultation with my pilot, decided to return via Bardsey Island which gave us a wide a berth as possible to Snowdonia. I accordingly gave Sergeant Ruffell a course for Bardsey Island, and once again we came safely back over base. By now the cloudbase was very low, and in the circumstances the pilot stated that the landing approach would be very shallow. This could result in a bumpy landing and he advised us to strap ourselves in. I had found the left strap, and was trying to locate the other one. The last thing I could remember was seeing the runway lights dead ahead, then a complete blank until I came to.

I was being lifted through a hole in the fuselage, then laid carefully on the ground next to someone else. People were moving around and I could hear voices. Someone said 'Don't worry about him, he's a gonner'. Until that moment I did not appreciate what had happened, but when I turned my head I could see, illuminated by vehicle headlights, the Anson standing on its nose at an angle of about sixty degrees. In fact Anson EF952 had hit the roof of Warren Farm with its starboard wing on the approach to runway 21. The son of the farmer was sleeping in the affected bedroom, but was uninjured. On reaching Station Sick Quarters I was placed on a table and all my clothes cut off as it was feared that I may have spinal injuries. Flight Lieutenant Graham gave me a couple of jabs in the arm, saying something about sleep, and I woke several hours later. Then I was moved along with Sergeant Richards, the staff wireless operator to Bryn Beryl, the naval sick bay of HMS Glendower, Pwllheli, (now Butlins, Pwllheli) where X-rays revealed no spinal injuries, and we were transferred to RAF Cosford. The staff wireless operator had damaged his spinal cord, although it was hoped that he would make a full recovery, I never knew the outcome. When I returned to Llandwrog I learned the fate of the others. The pilot and Sergeant Melvin, the bomb-aimer, had been thrown through the windscreen and both killed. Sergeant C.H.Cornell, the pupil wireless operator was not seriously injured, though his face was later rebuilt, but the door had jammed and until rescued he had lived in acute fear of an explosion or fire, which affected him long afterwards.' Sergeant Cornell married a local girl, but it is sad to relate that he lost his life while fishing in Caernarvon Bay after the war, where many of his wartime comrades perished. His body was later washed up on the beach opposite the farm where he crashed.

Bill Benton was later passed fit for flying duties and was posted to No.295 Squadron at Hurn, a founder squadron of 38 Group formed to carry out airborne operations associated with the invasion of Europe. After D-Day, they converted from Albemarles to Short Stirlings which dropped supplies and agents to resistance groups in western Europe. He reflects that his Anson crash meant that his eventual survival of the war in the air was enhanced because he missed being sent to Bomber Command at the time of its highest losses, in late 1943-44.

Bill Benton, survivor from Anson EF952 on 28th August 1943.

Warren Farm, a hazard in line with runway 21 at Llandwrog.

Chapter Six

Wireless Operator – Air

It has been said that the worst place in the world for a wireless operator to function was in an aircraft. In the Avro Anson the operator sat in a tiny cubicle behind the navigator, with the R1155 receiver and T1154 transmitter installation inches away from him. In fact, in any accident, he could sustain severe injuries to his head from hitting the control knobs of the transmitter. He had to listen for elusive signals through heavy static and the roar of the engines. It might be thought by the casual observer that the duties of an airborne wireless operator were not onerous, and that all that was required was to be on watch in case of emergency situations, or to pass round the flask of coffee. In fact he kept a log from the moment he sat down, plugged in his headphones, and checked his equipment. The headphones never came off except if the intercom became faulty, when messages were passed by hand, or for a quick visit to relieve himself.

The transmitter and receiver installation which equipped the Ansons each contained several thermionic valves, the filaments of which, as in a light bulb, did not like being knocked about as in a heavy landing. Also the majority of resistors were mainly a carbon type, prone to deteriorate when hot. The power feed to the sets came via carbon pile regulators which often became faulty, feeding excessive voltage with consequent damage. Reliability in the air therefore was questionable, and there were many failures, some with tragic results from a knock-on effect that bearings could not be taken. In fact, when Gordon Leigh was posted to Llandwrog as Sergeant in charge of radio servicing (and MR Team member) he opened one hut door to find it stacked from floor to ceiling with faulty sets. As a result several Ansons were unserviceable. In the air, apart from a valve change, little could be done to faulty equipment, since the circuitry was complicated for its day and inaccessible except in a workshop.

The navigator training AFU Ansons at Llandwrog always carried a wireless operator, principally to assist the navigator when required. This was usually a staff W/OP, but those under training would fly with a staff wireless operator on board until they were considered proficient enough to handle the duty on their own. Their training would have ensured that they passed a test of sending and receiving letters and figures at a speed of 22 words per minute from a school such as Yatesbury. They would be posted to a Signals School at airfields such as Madley, near Hereford, where they would gain basic experience in de Havilland Dominie or Percival Proctor aircraft learning to obtain life saving bearings.

Denis Travis arrived at Penrhos for an 8 week course in July 1942, moving on to Llandwrog for night flying. On completion of the course he was recommended for instructor duties as a staff wireless operator until he obtained a posting for operational duties some 14 months later. 'In good weather we would carry out two trips of 2½ to 3 hours per night with a two hours break for a meal, these after briefing as to the routes and stations available for bearings. This was very tiring for all the crew after a few nights, and could lead to mistakes. There were many flights over the sea without visual navigational aids. The 'Milk Run' was a good example, since the navigator would have to use DR (dead reckoning). On the heading almost due north from Fishguard towards the Isle of Man, the wireless operator would be kept busy taking a series of three bearings from base to give their position and allow a determination of true airspeed and the effect of winds. On one of these flights at night the pupil navigator approached me and asked what I thought the lights to port were. I replied that there should be none. When I looked out I realised that it was Dublin and concluded that the navigation was far adrift. When I went forward I realised I was wrong. The pilot was fast asleep! We had been drifting steadily to port in a dangerous situation. It was the second trip that night, in a busy week, and we were all tired.

Should a pilot feel that a trainee navigator was unsure of his position (in other words lost!), he would ask the wireless operator for a 'Fix'. This was obtained from a group of three radio stations, one of which would act as control. They would each measure the bearing of the signal from the aircraft and feed back its position via the controlling station. This was a failsafe situation, only generally used in an emergency.'

Over land at night, at a safe height and with reasonably good visibility, the navigation should have been straightforward. There were flashing white beacons, known as Occults, situated along, or near to the coastline of Britain. Aircrew were kept up to date with the codes used, and these were of great value in clear weather. Airfields each had a permanent two letter code which was sent out continually in Morse from red Pundit beacons which were often situated just off the airfield (in case of enemy activity) in a known position. Llandwrog used the code LW, and the other AFU in the area, Mona was MU. The most common request from a wireless operator to base was for a QDM. This is the code for a request for a magnetic reciprocal bearing, or a compass course to steer for the pilot to bring them back over base, or asked of another airfield if their own was fog bound.

Another, more unusual, activity for the wireless operator was the handling of carrier pigeons, which were taken on some flights. Should a ditching take place with no time to radio a position, then the pigeon could be released from the dinghy with this information. This practice was eventually discontinued when the local hawks latched onto the easy plump prey. Two pigeon lofts at Llandwrog were situated close to the crew briefing huts.

The wireless operator's duties would include reporting the position of the aircraft to base from time to time. Should they not report, then Llandwrog would try to make contact. In this way the airfield control officer had a last known position and heading for each aircraft aloft. The operator would also listen out on the distress frequency (6,440 Kcs) at three minutes after a quarter past, and three minutes after a quarter to the hour. Should there be a sudden warning of bad weather approaching, then the code BBA (Bring Back Aircraft?) would be sent to all aircraft to return to base immediately. Navigators, advised of this message by the wireless operators, would then have to quickly work out a course for home and safety. The last duty of the wireless operator prior to landing at night or in cloudy conditions was to obtain a reading of the barometric pressure at base to enable the pilot to check his altimeter. This was essential in the case of Llandwrog with its proximity to the mountains.

Llandwrog staff wireless operators Ken Coward left, and Denis Travis. *D.J. Travis*

Chapter Seven

Bomb Aimer Training

In an RAF operational bomber the bomb aimer would suddenly blossom into the VIP on board for a few minutes as the target was approached. The whole purpose of this hazardous flight was to carry their bomb load to this point, and release it with the expertise of this crew member. He would set up the complicated bomb sight and guide the pilot with minute corrections until the moment he pressed the bomb release. All this was carried out while the aircraft was rocked, or hit, by flak, and subject to attack by enemy fighters. The rest of the crew waited impatiently, hoping that he would get it right first time and they would not have to endure a dangerous re-run, severely reducing their chances of survival. He was not a passenger for the rest of the flight but, as a trained air gunner, would man the front turret. The moments when he moved over to the bombsight then were the most vulnerable to head on fighter attacks from any Luftwaffe pilots brave enough to attack through their own flak.

Peter North was one of many trained in Canada, at Lethbridge for bomb aiming and gunnery, then on to No.2 AOS at Edmonton for map reading and oblique photography. The latter course was essential to enable targets to be picked out, and for them to be photographed after the bombs hit, so that the accuracy and effectiveness of the operation could be determined back at base. He recalls arriving back in Britain:

'I was posted to Penrhos in September 1943 where two or three bomb aimers would fly in an Anson with a staff pilot, who would also carry out the navigation to well known bombing ranges. At Hell's Mouth we flew at a height of around fifty feet to the off shore targets, which came and went in a flash. The low level bombsight was a tangle of matchwood, with a pin at each corner, mounted on a tube of wood. Everything depended on the angle of your head and wrist. On moving to Llandwrog for night flying, life became serious. Very different from Canada, where the night navigation mainly consisted of turning left at the next set of traffic lights in a prairie town! At Llandwrog we started flying as crews, working together as a team. It was an uncomfortable feeling flying from this airfield. One second we were on the runway, the next over the sea, or mountains. I flew with a Canadian navigator who missed the Isle of Man completely and, when searchlights sprung into the sky ahead, we realised we were near the Irish coast. The navigator was arguing with the pilot, saying that it must be the Isle of Man. The pilot had the sense to take over the navigation and turn back and land at Jurby, short of fuel. There were Infra Red (IR) targets situated at Jurby and Douglas, as well as on the railway bridge at Conway.

The Bombsight Mark IX, with variations, was used in the Anson, and at least three hands would have been useful to work it. It was basically a compass with gearing so that the heading of the aircraft was shown on the sights. It contained two spirit levels, one for fore and aft, and one for lateral. It had a height bar in which a number of metal slides were placed, depending on the weight and type of bombs on board, each type having its own aerodynamics. There was a cross piece on which was set the wind speed and direction, and which moved the foresight to left or right of the heading. The target would appear between the drift wires, moving from front to rear. The bomb aimer would then call corrections to the pilot on the intercom 'Left Left!' etc. Quite crude; there we were, lying full length in the nose of the Anson, fumbling in the night, watching two spirit levels, with one eye on the target coming down the drift wires, and trying to keep one's head absolutely rock steady. The slightest movement and the bombs would drop well ahead or beyond the target.'

At the Hell's Mouth ranges trainee air bombers would start the high altitude bombing at an altitude of 6,000 feet with smoke bombs. Only when they were proficient at that height would they be allowed to bomb at 10,000 feet, where a miscalculation could place the delivery on land. Those who passed this test could then proceed to drop live bombs in the area reserved for this out in Cardigan Bay.

Air Training Corps cadets were found seats for these flights during their summer camps. One of them, Glyn Pritchard, of No.418 (Aberconway) Squadron recalls: 'At Penrhos on 26th June 1944 I was taken up in Anson MG650 by Flight Sergeant Sanders, RNZAF, and two bomb aimers. I sat by the pilot and operated the undercarriage cranking handle. As soon as we reached the range with the bomb aimer in position the pilot started to shout, hustle, and press him to drop the bombs, this happening four or five times before the second man's turn came. I felt that the pilot, on his own initiative, was giving these trainees a taste of operational urgency. Having dropped all the bombs the bomb aimers returned to the back of the aircraft. Then the pilot told me to change places with him and hold the controls, and I flew the Anson in gentle circles for some 20-30 minutes. Before he too went to the back for a smoke with the others he offered me a cigarette from a yellow packet of Gold Flake, which I gladly refused for there was talk that an Anson which had blown up in the area was because the crew had been smoking.' One presumes that this cadet, while enjoying the experience of being in temporary control of an Anson, kept his parachute close by him.

Bomb aimer at his post in an operational Lancaster of 619 Squadron. *Chas Bowyer*

Sergeant Peter North sampling the delights of Pwllheli in 1943.

Chapter Eight

The Ditchings

The mountains were not the only hazard faced by aircrew based at Llandwrog. Situated on a narrow peninsula there was the proximity of the sea to all three runways, and especially the east/west runway which finished a few yards from the beach. This resulted in aircraft ditching on take off, or after an overshoot on landing. The former is well illustrated by Anson EF978 which took off from the northwest runway in the early hours of 8th September 1943. After leaving the glare of the flare path, the pilot found himself with no instrument lights to fly by. The aircraft hit the dyke surrounding the airfield, and dropped into the sea on the other side. The rescue services were quickly on the scene and helped four of the crew from the surf, but the fifth member could not be revived by the time he was found. Several airmen had the misfortune to ditch on more than one occasion. One of these was Flight Sergeant G.J.Smith, who made a forced landing in the sea near Fort Belan in Anson N4884 on 24th October 1941. On 8th August 1942 he was the pilot of Anson DJ125 which crashed into the sea on take off from Llandwrog. Only LAC A.T.W.Walker, the air bomber, survived from the crew of five. A Canadian pilot, Pilot Officer T.F.Watt survived a ditching in Anson N4922 off Llandwyn Island on 9th May 1942, only to lose his life one month later on 10th June, with Pilot Officer J. M. Snow, when Anson N4983 dived into the sea on approach to Llandwrog. There are other instances of this pattern; clearly you usually only had one chance of a ditching survival.

On the wider scene, the navigation flights took place often with lengthy sea crossings, where any malfunction far from land could result in a ditching. Llandwrog lost more aircraft to the sea than the mountains. Some Ansons took off into the blue, never to be heard of again. Dinghy drill was an essential part of the training, practising how to evacuate the aircraft in the water and climb into a dinghy in heavy, wet, flying suits. After donning a parachute harness, the wearing of a Mae West life jacket was mandatory.

The opportunity of relating the story of two ditchings, one in daylight and one at night, are now taken from personal contact with the aircrew involved. Staff pilot Jack Stephenson recalls:

'The 16th October 1944 dawned bright and clear, Met forecast good. My briefing was to coordinate a sprog (novice) crew of navigator, bomb aimer, and wireless operator on a navigation exercise around the Irish Sea with the objective of developing confidence in their ability to get from A to B without getting lost. We took off in Anson DJ621 and climbed to an operational height of 7,000 feet on course to Fishguard. This leg was uneventful, then we turned north towards the Calf of Man, off the Isle of Man, where there was an infra-red target for the bomb aimer to have fun with. The sea below was dotted with fishing vessels and we settled to this long leg which would produce some interesting changes of course as the navigator's dead reckoning required. In this case we were soon off course to the west and closing with the southwest tip of Ireland. While I was considering how long to let this situation develop, the port propeller suddenly took off and raced ahead of us. I immediately shut the engine down, but at the same time the cowling blew off followed by the cylinders. In no time at all I was minus a complete engine. We lost some height while I got the aircraft under control and trimmed to offset the missing engine. By this time we were close to the Irish coast and the thought crossed my mind whether to make a forced landing there and risk being interned. However, I had planned to be married on the 28th October and did not wish to disappoint the lady. With a height of 5,000 feet I asked Llandwrog for a QDM, the magnetic course to fly home. It came as a bit of a shock to find that, after all the single engine practise I had done, the aircraft would not maintain height and we would have to ditch. The crew had been trained on how to exit the Anson and were quite calm when I informed them of our plight. A 'Mayday' had been transmitted and several aircraft on the exercise altered course to meet us plus the Air/Sea rescue launch set out from Fort Belan near the airfield. We were down to 1,500 feet, and out of sight of land when we sighted an aircraft carrier steaming south towards us. I suppressed thoughts of landing on her deck, and the wireless operator signalled her with a request to land alongside. We received 'RK' 'Carry on', and I turned to ditch slightly ahead on the lee side.

In that instant I recalled what a friend had told me of his own experience, that God was his co-pilot, but at the end only God was in control, which I repeated to myself a few seconds before we hit. The nose went under the water and I thought we were going straight to the bottom. Fortunately it had been a copybook landing and we surfaced and floated quite happily. The crew were magnificent, launching the dinghy and stepping into it without even getting wet. Soon a longboat from the carrier was on its way over to pick us up, and we sent off a Very flare to indicate to the ship and our fellows in the sky above that all was well. I went back inside the Anson for my cap and to look at the damaged engine mounting from the cockpit for the inevitable investigation. We were then taken in tow and were taken on board the carrier for hot baths to calm the shivers of the after effects of shock. The ship turned out to be the *Argus*, an

Staff pilot Jack Stephenson, kneeling centre, survivor from Anson DJ621, and wireless operators Jack Jeffries, Norman Fazackerly, and Bill Jackson. The other pilot standing right, is Geoff Kershaw who later lost his life in the Pennines flying as a civilian pilot post-war. *M Bryan*

Anson DJ621 over Anglesey in 1943. Ditched 16th October 1944. *Ken Coward*

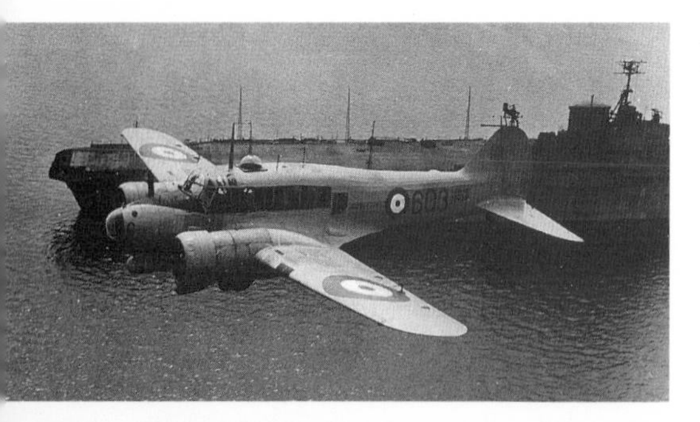

Anson flying over aircraft carrier. *Harry Holmes*

Crew of ditched Anson DJ618 on 28th March 1943. L-R: back row, Sgt. D.J.Travis P/O. G.S.C.MacLean, LAC L. Lambert. Front row, LACs Boustead, P.Gordon. *D.J.Travis*

old carrier which was on its way to scrapyards on the Thames. We then spent several happy days cruising with the Royal Navy. The rescue launch had come alongside for us but the captain refused to stop the ship again. As our Anson did not want to sink, it suffered the ignominy of being sunk by gunfire from the carrier crew who enjoyed the practise.' Losing their usually faithful steed like this must have seemed to the crew like shooting the family dog for going lame in one leg!

At 2100 hours on 28th March 1943, Anson DJ618 took off from Llandwrog with a crew of five, Pilot Officer G.S.C.Maclean the Canadian pilot, Sergeant D.J.Travis the staff wireless operator, with two pupil navigators and a bomb aimer. LAC L.Lambert was acting as first navigator, plotting courses and advising the pilot of these. LACs Boustead and P.Gordon completed the crew. They flew to Catterick in Yorkshire, across to Carlisle, then to the Isle of Man, and turned for home. Suddenly they ran into a terrible storm quite unexpectedly. Visibility was nil, and Travis was kept busy obtaining radio bearings (QDMs) to take them back to base. As they approached the coast the pilot was wary of the mountains beyond and, not being able to see the ground, backed off. Soon they became lost and, with fuel running low were losing height gingerly to 500 feet when the crew sighted lights from what appeared to be a large railway station. (This was in fact Holyhead harbour, where they were reported as an aircraft in distress by the coastguard on duty).

With petrol gauges showing empty, MacLean told the crew to take up crash positions and decided to land just as the engines spluttered to a stop, and the aircraft ditched in the sea at 90 mph. This was a great surprise to all since they thought they were over land. Travis pushed the separate packed dinghy into the sea but was unable to inflate it since he was blocking the exit for others of the crew, and the Anson was sinking fast. They all jumped into the water and for a short time clung to the aircraft. The pilot then swam round the dinghy and inflated it, cutting it loose at the same time. Luckily it was the right way up and MacLean was inside it. He was able to help Gordon in, but for the others it became a fight for survival. This was because the crew had their parachute harnesses on and, with numbed hands unable to release them, were incapable of inflating their Mae Wests to keep afloat. Travis made a determined effort and succeeded in climbing in next. It then became a life or death struggle for Lambert and Boustead since the three in the dinghy were exhausted and for a few moments it seemed as if they had lost one as they tried to hang onto his heavy flying suit. Luckily they had come down north-east of the Skerries and had some shelter from the land. With the heavy rain and gales the crew spent a cold and miserable night constantly baling, never seeming to gain on the several inches of water in the dinghy with only a drinking mug to use. They had no idea of their position, whether it was north or south of the Lleyn Peninsula. In the meantime the emergency kit had been drawn on board. This was a canister that contained a little food, water, medical supplies, and Very cartridges. The pistol however was not found until daylight in the water under their feet. The crew were heartened when a merchant ship flying a kite balloon was sighted not far away, so a succession of Very flares were fired. All to no avail, the ship sailed merrily on its way. Soon afterwards though the sight of the high bow wave of a Naval rescue launch cheered the airmen. HMS *Torch*, ML250, commanded by Lieutenant Commander H.S.Eaton, RNVR, soon had them aboard. They were whisked to the captain's cabin, undressed, given a shot of rum and whisky, wrapped in warm blankets and put to sleep in bunks. The captain told them that he had shaken 40 knots out of the launch on sighting their signals. On landing at Holyhead, the crew were taken to RAF Valley for a hot bath before being returned to Llandwrog. It had been the coldest night of their lives.

All the crew later went on to operational squadrons. Len Lambert was badly injured over the Ruhr in a Halifax aircraft. On returning to duty, on the night of 30/31 March 1944, almost exactly a year after the ditching, he took part in the disastrous raid on Nuremberg. Ninety-six aircraft were lost along with the lives of 545 aircrew. Lambert's Halifax was attacked by night fighters while turning onto the bomb run. He baled out along with the wireless operator and bomb aimer when this was indicated on the emergency signals, surviving to become prisoners of war. The pilot, Cyril Barton, however continued the run and personally released the bombs. He then nursed the aircraft back to Britain, and attempted a landing on one engine. Barton was killed in the subsequent crash, but the flight engineer and the two air gunners survived. The pilot was posthumously awarded the Victoria Cross.

Sergeant P.Gordon, a Canadian, was bomb aimer in a Lancaster returning from a bombing raid on Mannheim on 23rd September 1943. When the aircraft of 57 Squadron was hit by flak the pilot, Flying Officer Joe Hogan RCAF, tried to ditch in the River Seine in Paris. The blazing Lancaster exploded before this could be accomplished, but his actions saved many lives, with no injuries to civilians, though he was unable to save himself or his crew. A plaque commemorates this sacrifice on the wall of a store in the Rue de Rivoli, opposite the Louvre.

Anson N9551, from Penrhos, which hit an obstacle while low-flying over the sea on 2nd September 1941. Seen here being recovered at Aberdovey. *Tom Yates*

Chapter Nine

Personnel Photofile

Following a talk on the aircraft crashes of Snowdonia to members of the International Friendship League, the writer was given two autograph books by Miss Hope Roberts, formerly of Boston House, Llandudno. In the war years her parents accommodated many airmen from the nearest airfields during weekend passes, many being from Llandwrog. Mrs Roberts was known as 'Mumsie' and Hope as 'Hopeless". The books are a microcosm of wartime aviation history with autographs of many airmen, some of whom died soon after inscribing a few choice words. A few left valuable photographs in the albums. This chapter is included to share some of those pages, dated where known, with the reader, along with photographs from other sources.

Sergeant Trevor M. Blakemore, RNZAF, a staff pilot at Penrhos for a time. After a course at No.1 SPTU at Cark on Morecambe Bay he was posted to Llandwrog. On 14th November 1942 he took off with four crew on a night navigation exercise in Anson DJ628, never to return. The aircraft came down in the sea and two bodies were later washed up, but the other three, including Blakemore were never found. *Arthur Arculus*

Pilot Officer J. W. Croudis, RNZAF. On the night of 1st March 1943 this staff pilot took off in Anson EG129 on a night navigation exercise with four crew. Five minutes later the aircraft suffered an engine failure, and stalled after recovering from the initial dive. All on board lost their lives when it fell onto the banks of the Afon Llyfni near Penygroes. *Dave Roberts*

Staff pilot Pilot Officer Barry Fleming. On 28th April 1943 he survived a mountain crash in Anson EF823. (see 'Fallen Eagles'). News of his survival came through to his friend George Bates, whose best man he had arranged to be, during the wedding reception. Fleming survived the war to fly as Captain with British Midland Airways out of Coventry. He was tragically killed not in the air, but by a drunken driver at Christmas 1974. *Hope Roberts*

Wedding photograph of staff pilot Warrant Officer E. D. (Foggy) Fogden, RAAF, from Sydney on left. Observer Flight Sergeant F.N.Hamood, RAAF, from Geelong is on right. Later they went together to No.466 Squadron at Leconfield. On the night of 15/16th August 1943 they flew on a minelaying operation to St.Nazaire in Wellington LN442, reported missing, their fate is unknown. *Hope Roberts*

Wedding photograph in Edinburgh, 1942, of staff pilot Pilot Officer Laurie Howard RAAF from Perth, Western Australia with bride Jean, and George Bates as best man. Howard was later posted to Coastal Command and lost his life in a Sunderland flying boat which was shot down by the crew of a Junkers Ju 88. *George Bates*

Staff pilot Sergeant S. P. James, pilot of Anson AX407 from Llandwrog which made a forced landing in the sea on 1st May 1943. He lost his life along with his crew of four. *Hubert Scrivener*

Staff pilot Sergeant Geoff Maunders, left, with staff wireless operator Denis Travis on 20.2.43. Travis survived a ditching (see chapter 8). Maunders was posted to 101 Squadron where, as a German speaker, he became an extra crew member on the Lancasters transmitting messages to confuse Luftwaffe fighters and their ground control. He lost his life when his aircraft was shot down over Dusseldorf on 3rd November 1943, and is buried at Rheinberg. *Hope Roberts*

Sergeant Richardson, top right, in June 1942, staff wireless operator at Llandwrog. Later posted to 106 Squadron, he was killed on 30th March 1944 during the Nuremburg operation when 96 aircraft were lost because the attack was made in moonlight above white clouds so fighters were able to exact a terrible toll. He is buried at Hotten in the Ardennes. *D. J. Travis*

This photograph was the precursor of a tragedy with Anson MG111 from Llandwrog. This aircraft took off on 20.11.43., flown by Sergeant J. Szczerbaty, a Polish pilot, for an air to air firing practice over Hell's Mouth Bay at 1035 hours. After this the weather deteriorated rapidly and they flew into cloud, striking the rocks near the summit of Craig Cwm Silyn at 1100 hours. AC2 Herbert. H. Sutton, a policeman from Ilford who had volunteered for aircrew, (back row 1st left), AC2 P. A. Shields (front row 2nd left), and AC2 R. Ross, (front row far right), all lost their lives along with the pilot and gunnery instructor Flight Sergeant J. Davis. *J.Sutton*

Frank Taylor, a Scot, who trained as an airgunner at Penrhos in 1940. He was shot down and made a prisoner of war in February 1942. On resuming his acting career after the war one of his roles was in the stage version of 'Oklahoma' with Howard Keel. He later made his home in Sydney and his many roles included Sergeant 'Scotty' Macleod in the television series 'Division 4.' *Evan L. Jones*

BERRIE BINDER TRAVIS
SMALL RICHMOND KIRKHAM TOMMIE
Nº 5 COURSE, WOP/AGs.

Sergeant (later Warrant Officer) L. 'Jock' Tommie, in September 1943, staff wireless operator at Llandwrog. Shortly before, on 23rd August, he was aboard Anson N5371 which crashed on Foel Fras, though all the crew survived. He was posted to No.103 Squadron, Elsham Wolds, and lost his life in a Lancaster during an operation against Stuttgart on 26th July 1944. He is buried in Le Grand Cemetery, Orleans.

Typical wartime scene under the Mostyn Street Clock, in Llandudno. Sergeants Sidney Foster, Jim Haskett, & Terry Walkden on a weekend pass.

Staff pilot Flight Sergeant Ben Vye, RCAF, of Newcastle, New Brunswick. On the night of 22/23rd September 1942 he took off on a night navigation exercise in Anson DJ126 from Llandwrog. He and his crew lost their lives when the aircraft hit the southern slopes of Cairnsmore of Fleet, near Wigtown, while flying just 5 degrees off course. *Hope Roberts.*

Last resting place of Flight Sergeant Ben Vye in Kirkinner Cemetery, Wigtown.
Gilbert Rothery

Section Officer Joan Roman, senior WAAF at Llandwrog in 1945, and wife of General Pierre Roman, leader of the Free Belgian Forces.

Hill walkers dwarfed by the Glyder range. *Gordon Leigh*

Part II

The Birth of the RAF Mountain Rescue Service

'Great things are done when men and mountains meet.'
William Blake

Craig Yr Ysfa. Site of the first high ground crash in Snowdonia.
Gordon Leigh

Chapter Ten

The Beginning

Before the Flood

With the benefit of hindsight, several airfields constructed in the proximity of mountainous areas would not have been built. The saving in cost of aircraft and even more, of aircrew lives, would have been considerable, though there still would have remained the problem of alternative sites. Before, and during the early years of the Second World War, there were few high ground aircraft crashes. Pilots generally shunned these areas, since one was unlikely to survive a forced landing on the hostile terrain. Much of the navigation was by map reading in daylight, and potentially dangerous areas were thus avoided by flying round them. Any accidents which did occur were dealt with by the nearest RAF station, whose aircraft it often was. Aircraft en route for training at Penrhos would usually fly via Sealand, which would keep them clear of high ground in north Wales.

The first high mountain crash in Snowdonia was that of Blenheim L9039 from No.13 OTU, Bicester, on a cross country flight on 9th April 1940. It struck the rocks of Craig Yr Ysfa (Eerie Rocks) in cloud, in level flight at 3,000 feet with such force that the propeller hubs were embedded in the hard granite. Sergeant A.E.Hall and his three crew members were killed outright. Following this there was only a small build up in crash incidence through 1941, but mid 1942 brought a greatly increased level of aircraft activity (see Appendix F), including those operating at night from Llandwrog. Also, by August, aircraft of the USAAF were starting to appear in substantial numbers, and would add to the accident statistics in the area for the rest of the war. There were few American survivors.

The Beginning

On 13th May 1942, a lucky day for some, Flight Lieutenant George D. Graham, was posted to RAF Llandwrog as the Station Medical Officer. He soon became acutely aware of the lack of any organisation to search for and rescue any victims of high ground crashes. Quite recently, on 21st April his predecessor had attended Anson N4980 which had crashed the previous night on the summit ridge of the Carneddau range, close to an altitude of 3,000 feet, with the loss of one of the trainee navigators. It may well having been told of this incident in such a remote place, which took hours to reach, which stirred him into a plan of action, or he was possessed of great foresight. By the end of June he had started a small team of volunteers comprising himself as leader, since he had extensive climbing experience including the Swiss Alps, and a few medical orderlies and attendants from the Station Sick Quarters (SSQ) with MT drivers. Thus any crash victims found alive would benefit immediately from their life saving expertise. When large scale operations were required, the team could be backed by a party of administrative and general duties personnel to assist with searching and carrying any casualties

One of the latter was flight mechanic Noel Bailey who arrived at Llandwrog in October 1941, and recalls, 'The Tannoy would request some 10-15 volunteers to attend mountain crashes when these started occurring. I remember the Hudson on Snowdon, absolutely disintegrated, unrecognisable as an aircraft, whereas Ansons generally were. In the worst crashes Flight Lieutenant Graham asked us to collect all human remains and bring them to him. I was not sickened as some, but just had a great feeling of sadness. What a waste of young lives, some from as far away as Australia and New Zealand, killed before they had a chance for combat. I found one young airman in a sitting position by a rock, his blond hair blowing in the breeze, quite dead.'

Andrew Roberts was another flight mechanic at Llandwrog, a fortunate posting, since his home was in Caernarvon. 'I can remember my first call out quite clearly. The cloud level had been low all day and, as night fell, it started to rain continuously. When a crash was reported I was roped into the rescue team and in no time at all I was on a lorry, part of a small convoy weaving its way through Caernarfon and into the mountains. Eventually the vehicles stopped and in the dim light of masked headlights I could see a farmer and his dog standing by a gate. He had found the engines of the aircraft at the foot of a mountain after hearing a crash. (Presumably Anson LT184 on Mynydd Perfedd on 5th October 1943). He offered to be our guide in a thickening, freezing mist. After an hour of searching my overcoat and boots were soaking and I was very tired. At this point the farmer took us all down to his farm (Maes Caradoc) where we were given tea by the farmer's wife in the warm kitchen, and waited for dawn. At first light the clouds had risen to the peaks and we resumed the search. As we wound our way over the wet scree the ropes, stretchers, and first aid kit we were carrying became very heavy. Hopes of finding the aircrew alive were dwindling. Eventually we reached a huge protruding rock which we edged round in single file. I was amazed to see the familiar Anson lying flat on the rock facing upwards as if the pilot had seen the rock face at the last moment in his frantic effort to gain height. The Anson seemed to be intact apart from the missing engines. As I came nearer I could see the crew sitting in their places as if they were dummies. There was no blood, nor was there any movement. All were dead. A Canadian airman was about my age and he seemed to be smiling. That smile has been etched in my memory ever since. I cried as we placed the bodies onto stretchers and strapped them down. The stretchers were then dragged and carried down the slippery slopes. As we travelled back through Caernarvon I saw my mother coming out of Boots the Chemist. I whistled and she waved back, knowing nothing of the dead young men who lay at my feet.'

Yet another flight mechanic roped into rescue operations was Walter Harvey, from County Antrim, at Llandwrog from early 1943 to late 1944.'I can't remember how many young airmen we carried down the moun-

Blenheim L9039 wedged in the cliffs of Craig Yr Ysfa *Ifor Hughes*

Author as school governor, takes pupils of Ysgol Ro Wen to Blenheim site in 1990, fifty years after the crash.

Llandwrog MR team prepare for a trip. Left to right: Corporal McTigue, Flight Lieutenant Graham, Corporal Jackson, LAC Cummings. *Daily Express*

The Battleground; though 'vertigo' would be a good title for this photograph of Foel Goch rising above the Nant Francon Pass and A5 road, with 3030ft Elidir Fawr beyond. *Gordon Leigh*

tains. When 'Duty Crew report immediately' announcement came over the Tannoy, it was nearly always another crash. We rushed to the mountains where the MRS would set up a base camp. We then proceeded to climb to the site of the crash, the going always tough and arduous. The bodies of the crew would be strapped to stretchers and, with as much dignity as was humanly possible on that awkward terrain, we started the long sad trek down. On one such search looking for bodies after a crash (Anson LT116 also on Mynydd Perfedd on 8th June 1944) we saw a body on a ledge. When it was recovered by the MR team, I had quite a shock, for I knew this airman well. It was Flight Sergeant Sullivan, an Australian pilot. Every time he saw me he always used to whistle the tune McNamara's Band, for he thought maybe I had Irish connections. I was late getting back to quarters, but my mates had laid out my best blues so I could catch up with them at a social evening arranged by Lord Newborough for all personnel. It helped to lessen the shock of what I had seen earlier.'

The Battleground

The area of operations of the team was roughly all 848 square miles of what is now the Snowdonia National Park, with occasional excursions beyond. It is the toughest country south of the Scottish Grampians and, in winter, a most hostile place. Apart from the coastal strip and lower valleys, the rest of the area is mountainous, with much of the high ground attaining an altitude well in excess of 1,000 feet, and indeed fourteen peaks exceeding an altitude of 3,000 feet, all in the northern section. The mountains are often craggy and remote; no place for a crash survivor to find succour. They were also remote from the would be rescuers. The highest peaks stand well back from access roads, as if wishing to distance themselves from all human activity. Even in the rare instance of the rescuers knowing the exact location of a crash, it could take several hours to reach the site. Having collected basic kit and food, then travelled by the nearest track to the base of a mountain, there may still have been over two thousand feet of climb, and some traversing, to accomplish in atrocious weather. Naismith's Rule states that it takes 1 hour to traverse 3 map miles, plus an extra ½ hour for every 1,000 feet of climb: this in good weather and not up scree or rock face. Usually many hours would elapse between the actual crash time and arrival of skilled help, every hour leading to a deterioration in the condition of any survivor.

More than 300 aircrew would lose their lives on these mountains. From near the north coast the National Park border runs south up the valley of the River Conwy, makes for beyond Bala, then curves round to capture the Aran range, before heading for the coast at Aberdovey. To the west, the peaks of Yr Eifl (The Fork Prongs, more usually known as the Rivals) would be visited both operationally, and for many training sessions. Strangely, the hostile and aloof central Snowdon massif itself would only collect seven of the one hundred aircraft which have crashed in the area to date. There were no survivors here, on this the highest section. The Carneddau range, crouching, unseen at night or in cloud, between homeward bound aircraft and their western bases, would cut down thirty five, or over a third of the total losses. Even today Snowdonia claims many accidents among hikers each year, some fatal, most on Snowdon itself.

Frustration

In the Operations Record Book for RAF Llandwrog on 29th November 1942 appeared the following summary by the Station Medical Officer 'During the last five months there have been 10 major crashes in the Snowdonia area from the Conway valley to the Rival mountains which this SSQ has attended over an area of 40 x 30 miles. Total dead 40, total injured removed to hospital 8.' This report may have been precipitated by incidents during November which added to the frustration of the team.

At 1200 hours on the 20th, Hawker Henley L3334, a target tower from RAF Towyn was reported as having crashed into the cliffs of

Craig Cym Silyn, scene of two crashes, and later site of a warning radio beacon.

Site of Anson N4981 which crashed on Moel Eilio on 20th November 1942. The Afon Gwyrfai seen far below meets the sea by Llandwrog airfield.

Craig Cwm Silyn, near Penygroes. Graham, with his infant team, set off promptly, only to find that the mountain was covered with an all enveloping mist. The same day the mist was the undoing of the crew of five of Anson N4981 from Penrhos which approached the hamlet of Betws Garmon, southeast of Caernarvon, from the coast, flying into a lowering mist and narrowing valley. The pilot, Sergeant A. E. Clay, could not see the pass through to Llyn Cwellyn and, with not enough room to turn round, chose to climb steeply away up the slopes of Moel Eilio which the Anson struck at 1435 hours. Villagers, who had observed the aircraft start its tragic climb and heard the crash, made their way up the steep mountain and reached the wreck an hour later, finding one airman still alive. The Llandwrog team were still searching for the Henley, and could not be contacted, so a party from the bomb storage depot at RAF Llanberis was called out, reaching the crash at 1800 hours, just as the survivor expired. Eventually it would be found that his injuries were not serious, and he had died of shock and exposure. The next day the Henley was seen rammed into a cliff face, Pilot Officer W. J. Havies having died instantly. This was in such a precarious position that local quarrymen, used to working on rock faces, were called in to recover the pilot's body, an embarrassing situation for the team. [This peak claimed Anson MG111 from Llandwrog, with its crew of five, exactly one year later to the day.]

Having been dispirited by these events, where they could have saved a life, worse was to come. Eight days later, Anson DJ635 piloted by Sergeant D. E. Johnson, an American in the RCAF, failed to return from a night exercise, the crew having acknowledged a recall to Llandwrog due to approaching bad weather. It was sighted next day high on the slopes of Foel Gron, a mile eastwards of the earlier Anson, having crashed at 1929 hours on the 28th. The report did not come in until 1400 hours, but the rescue team were on site by 1515 hours, tearing up the road to Bettws Garmon, like mad things. They then raced up from Llyn Cwellyn, little above sea level to 1,500 feet, like fell runners. The Anson had, almost maliciously, managed to find a wall to smash into in that remote spot, but the wireless operator, Sergeant C. Knight, was still alive. He had a sustained a compound fracture of his right leg, and was suffering from shock and exposure. He was rushed to the C & A Hospital at Bangor, but died the next day. The team had come so close to saving him, and perhaps others of the crew. Fellow staff pilot George Bates considers that the crew may have seen the large body of water of Llyn Cwellyn through a gap in the clouds and, thinking it was the Menai Strait, descended to what they thought was the flatlands of Anglesey beyond.

Shortly before midnight on 14th January 1943 came the most testing time for the team to date. Anson EG110, from Llandwrog, with four crew on board was reported overdue, and believed to have come down in the sea. Some air searches were carried out the next morning, but heavy cloud prevailed over the peaks. At 1530 hours came the dramatic news that Pilot Officer Ken Archer, the injured New Zealander pilot, had made his way down from the wreck to a remote farmhouse above the Conway valley. George Graham and his few medical orderlies rushed at breakneck speed, taking just an hour to reach the farm of Rowlyn Uchaf. While receiving first aid, Archer told them that the rest of his crew were badly injured, and could only identify the site as lying above two lakes. The MO and his small team set off up the Eigiau valley, turning off to follow the old miners track to Melynllyn to start the search as soon as Archer departed for hospital. They were joined much later by a large party of

LAC, later Sergeant F. H. G.Trimmer, who lost his life in Anson N4981. *J.Trimmer*

Sergeant, later P/O, Ken Archer in Llandwrog village. *D.J.Travis*

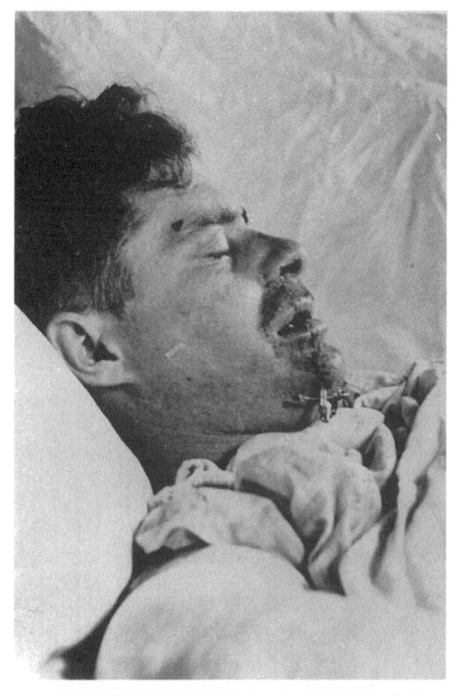

personnel from Llandwrog. The lorry bringing them however could not negotiate the steep hills and bends up to the plateau, and the party had to march the six miles up to the base set up at the Melynllyn hut. Here, already exhausted men, who were not mountaineers, had to climb another thousand feet onto the surrounding snow covered peaks in atrocious weather, and in greatcoats and ordinary RAF boots. A Beaufighter sent from No.456 Squadron at Valley dropped flares wide of the mark because there was no communication between the crew and the teams. These, urged on by a desperate Graham fought the elements until a snowstorm in the early hours forced a halt until daybreak. Never have RAF personnel striven so hard to save their own (a story told in detail in 'No Landing Place', along with other survivor stories). The next day the Anson was found high in a ravine on Foel Grach, with only the navigator, Sergeant Paterson, still alive. Even then the MO was in another team on Foel Fras and took over an hour to reach him. It is a miracle that Paterson survived the ordeal. It was not through a lack of endeavour that the others did not. This crash, more than any, brought to a head the many problems to be faced: the almost impossibility of night searches, the lack of communication, vehicles unsuitable for mountain terrain, lack of proper clothing or climbing boots, all influencing that crucial element, time.

The only glimmer of hope in all this tragedy was that Flight Lieutenant George Graham's efforts were eventually recognised by the Air Ministry with the award of an MBE for his services to mountain rescue in June.

Sergeant Frank Paterson, just after arrival in Llandudno Hospital. *Arthur Arculus*

Sergeant Frank Paterson on a better day. *Arthur Arculus*

Chapter Eleven

The Transformation

It took Flight Lieutenant George Graham many months of hard work through the spring of 1943 to convince the Air Ministry of the need for extra items for his team; this while carrying out his normal medical duties, attending further crashes, and holding training sessions in the mountains. Not only did he instruct in rudimentary climbing techniques, but the team spent many hours familiarising themselves with the various mountain ranges which had already interrupted the flight of aircraft, and were expected to do so again.

On 6th July 1943 Graham pronounced his new search and rescue team ready for operations, and commenced an incident log. (N.B. The team is variously named MR Team, Unit, or Service in records). The first entry was made on 6th July and the hour shows the keenness of the members. '0445 hours: A search exercise was commenced at this hour, the dummy crash being located at a point on the central peak of the Rival Mts. Three search parties were sent out from the Humber, which had followed the track from Llithfaen village to the gap between the two Northerly peaks reaching a height of 1,500 feet. Visibility above this height was nil owing to cloud and darkness. RT contact was maintained successfully between all parties to Humber base, and station base to Humber WT. After dawn the exercise was carried on to Porthdinllaen point, 14 miles direct from Llandwrog across the sea. WT contact was made.' The choice of the Rivals was prophetic for, on 3rd September 1944, the team would be called out to a Halifax which crashed on these very peaks.

The success of this exercise was in direct contrast to earlier communications problems. Graham now had constant control of his search parties. In the meantime, on 6th July, the exercise became a reality and at 0745 hours they were called to attend the crash of Lancaster R5736, from 1660 HCU, into a shallow hillside near Llangerniew on the Denbigh Moors. There were no survivors and they were obliged to search and account for all the crew members, the least satisfactory, but necessary part of their work. At first only three crew were found and an aircraft was requested from base to search for any opened parachutes in the area. This was speedily carried out with good communications between the team and the aircraft, but no trace of any crew bailing out was found. The team then was able to search the wreckage with confidence and found the remaining three bodies. The team returned to Llandwrog at 1800 hours.

The increasing interest by the higher echelons of the RAF are noted by the inspection of the MRS vehicles and unit by Air Commodore Keynes, Consultant of Surgery, RAF, and Wing Commander Forbes, SMO of No.25 Group on 20th July. They were closely followed on 6th August, by Wing Commander Ruffel Smith, of Flying Training Command, and Flying Officer Redwhite, of the RNZAF. The latter had a special interest in the unit, since airmen in New Zealand had also to contend with mountainous terrain, where the highest peak, Mount Cook, attains an altitude of over 12,000 feet. They were taken for a rescue demonstration to the Rivals, and treated to a not unusual visibility of 10 yards on the central peak.

By this time some progress had been made in equipment. Windproof clothing, ropes, maps, and compasses became avail-

Members of Llandwrog MR Team practice lowering a casualty down a rock face. Left to right: LAC Jackson, F/Lt Graham, Cpl Martin. *Daily Express*

Tommy (Jock) Cummings carrying a type 38 Radio transmitter/receiver. *Daily Express*

able, though standard service boots or wellingtons were still the only footwear. The Humber ambulance was now equipped with an Army tank 'Type 19' radio for WT (Wireless Telegraphy) communication to base at Llandwrog and facilitate contact with the 'Type 38' radios for voice communication, now carried by one member of each search party. These sets worked on a frequency of 7.4 to 9 MHz, designed with a weight saving combined HT/LT dry battery. Even so the complete unit weighed around 22 Lbs. When used with the 12 feet, three section aerial they gave a range of up to two miles. Where searches progressed through radio blackspots deep in the hills, the team learned to use a member on high ground as a relay station. The Humber was loaded with better medical supplies, splints, oxygen, heaters, and food. In October its roof was painted with black and yellow stripes to enable it to be easily seen by returning search parties and participating aircraft.

Further frustration

However, in August, there occurred another frustrating session for the members of the MR Unit. On the 29th, they were notified by Flying Control at 1700 hours that the crash of a Botha, from Hooton Park on the Wirral, had been located by the pilot of a sister aircraft south of Llyn Eigiau. An immediate response was made but, on reaching the Eigiau valley, the Jeep was brought to an abrupt halt by a ravine across the track (possibly the result of the dam burst in 1926) and the mountain HQ was set up at this point. The slopes over to Llyn Cowlyd were searched into the night, with no trace of the Botha. At 0500 hours on the 30th, the search recommenced all over 2622 feet Pen Llithrig-y-wrach in a gale and heavy rain, to no avail. At 0900 all parties returned to base for food, but two members were missing. All were subsequently found, though one had been injured, and brought

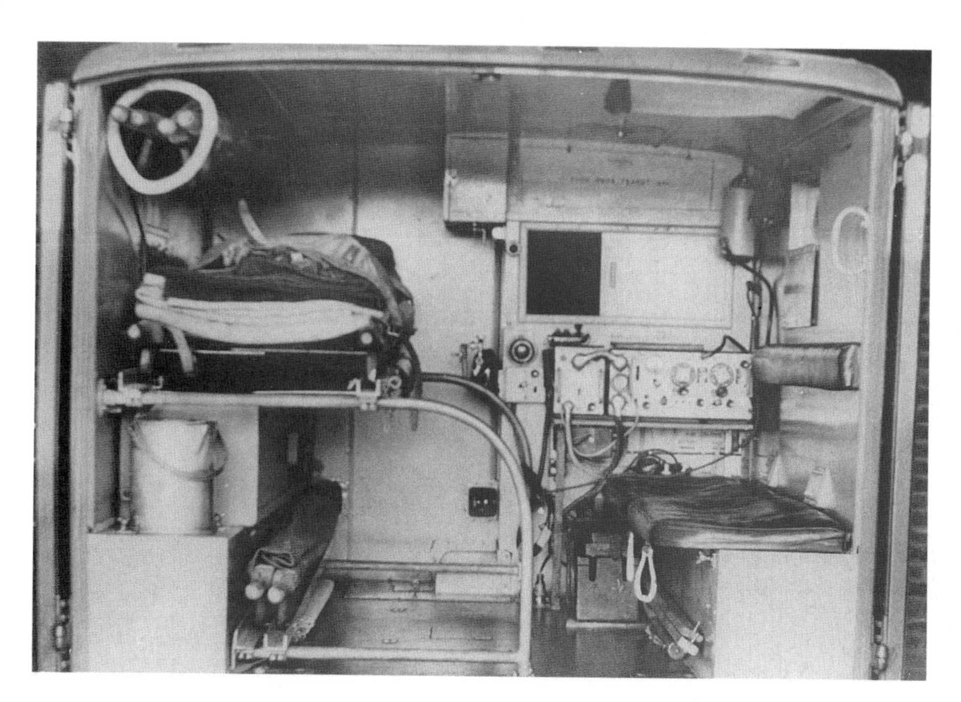

back. The MO returned to Llandwrog for more food and more accurate information. At 1200 hours a Police report came in that the crash had been found by the Home Guard on Cregiau Gleision, above Cowlyd. This was climbed first by a party under Pilot Officer Bowen and, on his return, by a determined Graham. Nothing was found. The next report, at 1800 hours, of the crash being located near Capel Curig, was found to be incorrect. At this point, Graham requested helpers from No.34 MU, of Bethesda, to search the western slopes of the Carneddau, while his team searched the eastern slopes. The latter made their way to the summit of Foel Grach by 2200 hours without finding the aircraft, and had to descend in cloud and darkness. Their only consolation was a ration of rum before all returned to Llandwrog at 0100 hours on the 31st. At 1200 hours another report came in that the crash had been sighted on Llywdmor, well to the west. Graham this time was able to carry out an air search, and saw the crash as reported, a few hundred feet below the rocky summit. This was reached at last at 1800 hours, the team having climbed past 'the bleached wreckage of the Junkers 88' (actually the Heinkel He 111), to find that the four crew of the Botha had died on impact. Extra personnel had been brought along to carry the bodies down, but they were not very fit at climbing such steep slopes. Darkness set in before the stretchers could be brought down so they were left until morning. On descending it was realised that

Interior of Humber ambulance complete with type 19 radio for communication with team members and base. *Dr T.O.Scudamore*

Blackburn Botha, three of which were lost to Snowdonia's hills. *BAe Brough*

the Jeep driver, Jock Cummings, who had been to base for more torches, was missing. He had returned to the mountain from the other side and missed them. The MO took a weary search party up this hard mountain again. A lonely Cummings was eventually seen 'As a pale flickering light among the rocks at the summit'. He was led down, having become exhausted after losing his bearings. They reached base at 0400, and were out again at 0900 hours on 1st September to recover the bodies. Flight Lieutenant Graham's entry on this effort signs off cryptically 'Thus ended the longest continuous operation in which the MR Unit had been

Sergeant G. M. Hepinstall, pilot of Botha L6202 which crashed on Llwydmor. His signet ring was found years later by ATC cadets and returned to his sister. *Mrs Winnie Hepinstall*

The Graveyard: The Carneddau range, including Pen Yr Ole Wen, Carnedd Davydd, and Carnedd Llewelyn, from Elidir Fawr. *Gordon Leigh*

employed. The long delay in finding the crash was entirely due to having been given a grossly inaccurate pinpoint.'

Graham and his team pushed their vehicles hard, always driving flat out and, as a consequence there were several accidents. On 5th October 1943 the Jeep, with Graham at the wheel, skidded on a corner in Bangor and went straight through a shop window. Having notified the police and cleared out the glass, the team went on its way to start a search.

On 3rd November the Air Ministry invited representatives of the Press to Llandwrog. Following an introduction at the Sick Quarters, photographers and reporters were transported to Cwm Silyn, near Penygroes. Here they were treated to the techniques involved with locating an aircraft crash, giving emergency medical aid, and transporting the injured down cliffs and thence to hospital. The resultant articles appeared in 'Picture Post' and national newspapers six days later. In print, the team appeared to be so organised, almost casual. From July 1942 to the end of 1943 the team rescued 39 survivors, the totals including the few who made their own way down but were given first aid by the team MO and orderlies.

The Graveyard

The real searches were a different matter, as evidenced by events at the end of November 1943. During the summer months the team had benefited from the interest and participation of another medical officer, Flying Officer Tom Scudamore. Arriving at Penrhos in May 1943, he was asked by the SMO, Squadron Leader A. Collins, to hold the sick parades at Llandwrog when Graham was fully occupied with mountain rescue activities. Scudamore and Graham got on well together and the former found himself being invited out on training exercises and rescues, though his only mountaineering experience was having been sent to the summit of Pen y Fan in mid-Wales by his college headmaster at Brecon as a yearly penance each Whit Monday.

At 1230 hours on 1st December, with Graham on leave, a call came through to Scudamore that an Anson from Jurby had crashed

The Graveyard: The Carneddau range, Pen Helig Ddu, and Carnedd Llewelyn.
Gordon Leigh

on the Carneddau the previous evening, and two crew had found their way down to Bethesda. Leaving the Sick Quarters in the capable hands of Sergeant Harvey, Scudamore set out with the team to Bethesda, only to find that Sergeants Knight and Gilbert, the pilot and wireless operator, had descended in cloud, and could not help with a position for the Anson. With just the knowledge that the aircraft had been flying from east to west, they headed for Llyn Ogwen and proceeded to search the eastern slopes of the mountains up to Carnedd Llewelyn. The team were up there in terrible weather most of the night, saved by the self heating tins of soup that they carried for a bit of internal warmth. The team went back to Llandwrog next morning to collect victuals. Graham was there! Someone had told him of the crash and he came whizzing back from leave. He told Scudamore 'You made a big mistake, you should not be above Ogwen, but searching the Graveyard!'

At this time LAC Reed from the missing Anson had also turned up at Bethesda, and confirmed Graham's predictions. This time Graham led the way to the Conway valley at top speed, and turned up to the Eigiau valley, and onto the rocky track to the Melynllyn hut.

Sergeant Tim Knight, pilot of Anson EF909.

Sergeant Roy Gilbert survivor from Anson EF909, left, at Jurby, with F/Sgt Jack Tennyson, who died in an Anson crash in Cumbria on 30th January 1944, and Sergeant Haydon. *R.Gilbert*

Corporal McTigue and LAC Jackson scan the slopes of Craig Cwm Silyn on 3rd November 1943. *Daily Express*

They hastened up the steep slopes onto the plateau between Foel Grach and Foel Fras. Graham said 'We will search here. This is the Graveyard'. The words were as good as 'Open Sesame' and the mist started to lift. There was the Anson just a quarter of a mile away. The remaining survivor LAC Thomson, of Clapham, was found alive tucked up in a parachute. As night fell he was carried down with some difficulty to the waiting ambulance. Another day on and the result would have been very different.

(The 'Graveyard' was an area within a radius of some 2½ miles of Llyn Dulyn where twenty aircraft would eventually be claimed.)

The story of this search and rescue was better than any fiction and the BBC got to hear of it. Realising that this would catch the imagination of the public, just two months later it was broadcast. While the script has not survived in the BBC archives, Canadian Tim Knight, the pilot of the Anson, obtained a copy. This is printed in its entirety in the following chapter (by kind permission of the BBC Copyright Department) to show a little of what the world at large was told of the MRS at the time.

Chapter Twelve

Into Battle

This series, on the wartime Forces Programme, told stories from various branches of the services. This particular contribution, No.255, was entitled 'Mountain Rescue', and was transmitted 9.20-9.30 pm on Saturday 29th January 1944. It was written by Donald Stokes, and produced by Brigid Maas. A recording was made from transmission for possible inclusion in overseas programmes. Standard script abbreviations are made:

FX. sound effects, **FU** fade up, **F/O** fade out.

FX.	F/U Drum Roll & 'Lillibulero'. Down for;
Announcer.	Into Battle. The Fighting Spirit of The United Nations.
FX.	Up 'Lillibulero' and out.

Announcer. There is one branch of the Royal Air Force of which little is known, the RAF Mountain Rescue Service. How it operates is shown in this story of a rescue carried out recently in the Welsh mountains.

Narrator. Because Britain today is one vast aircraft carrier, it follows that aircraft must operate over country dangerous to any aircraft that run into trouble. The mists and mountain peaks of the north and west, particularly, are a daily hazard to the many air crews and this is where the Mountain Rescue Service comes in. Day and night they stand ready for the emergency which calls them to perform their arduous and unusual task. The first intimation of trouble in this particular incident was the arrival of two airmen in a tiny Welsh hamlet near Bethesda, one morning last November.

FX. Faint knock on door. repeated. Door opens.

Woman. (Welsh accent, horrified) You poor man, whatever has happened, here come inside both of you. Lean on me, now, easy now. (calling) Glyn, go up on top and get your father. Tell him there are two men here, badly hurt, two RAF boys. Off you go. (To men) Here, sit down here, now your poor faces, they're cut to pieces. What has happened?

RAF man. (weakly) Plane......crashed.

Woman. What, near here, where is it?

RAF man. Long way....up mountain....to the east.

Woman. Are there any more of you, any more of the crew?

RAF man. Two others....still in plane...one is badly hurt.

FX. Music X/F Phone Bell.

Control. (phone distorted) Hello Medical Officer, this is Flying Control here. Will you stand by with your Mountain Rescue Unit. We have a report that an aircraft has crashed on a training flight. I'll give you the details.

Narrator: The unit raced across the country to the mountainous district where the aircraft had crashed. In charge was the

Medical Officer, Flight Lieutenant George Graham, MBE., with seven other men under him, all skilled mountaineers. They travelled in a special four-wheeled drive ambulance, carrying everything required for a rescue, from hot water bottle to complete surgical sets.

FX. F/U Big car engine in bottom gear: It stops: Up wind and music. Hold behind following.

Leader. All right men, we'll make base here. Ambulance won't go any farther. Now keep the map very clearly in your mind and keep in touch with base on the walky talky. Now is each party quite clear where to search?

Voices. Yes Sir.

Leader. Right. I wish this rain would stop. We'll probably find it's snowing higher up. But still we'll have an aircraft spotting for us directly it's light, but it's up to us to try and find the aircraft before then. There are two men still inside it, and we have no time to lose.

F/O FX.

Narrator. Each man of the three searching parties carried a small transmitting and receiving set called a walky talky which kept them in constant touch with each other, and with their base in the ambulance below, and through that with Flying Control. The parties set out, up the steep mountain face into a wilderness of rock and shale and icy, blinding rain. Each man had a powerful lamp strapped to his forehead, to guide his footholds on the crags and, from time to time, they sent up flares in hoping to catch a glimpse of the wrecked machine.

FX. F/U Music and wind: Swish of rocket from pistol.
Sect Ldr 1. (distort) Number one section here. No sign of any wreck.
Sect Ldr 2. Number two reporting. Cannot see wreck in this area.

Sect Ldr 3. No luck here.

F/O FX.

At one o'clock in the morning the leader called in the parties and told them they would start again at dawn. When the first light came an aircraft co-operated in the search.

FX. Plane's engines:

Observer. Aircraft calling ground. Nothing in sight on this peak, but cloud is very bad. Very difficult to make observation.

Leader. M.O. answering. Thank you. If the cloud gets any worse you'd better push off. We don't want to have to rescue you too.

F/O Aircraft.

Narrator. The weather became steadily worse and soon the aircraft had to abandon the search. Hour after hour the seven (i) men went on with their job; in their thick mountaineering kit, slowly and painfully scaling the slate crags, whose sharp edges cut the hands and made foot and handholds treacherous, investigating every crevice and gully which might hide man or machine. The microphone which was clamped to the throat of each man kept him in touch with the others, and with the waiting ambulance.

FX. F/U Music and Wind.

Jimmy (distort) Jimmy here. I've just got to the top of the crag at F-3-4. Can't see very far. This cloud is closing in.

Orderly. Any use going down the gully on the west side? I could work down there from where I am.

Jimmy. No there couldn't be any survivors if it hit the deck there. Where are you Jack?

Orderly. (distort) Working my way up the main face. There's a nasty bank of mist rolling up. Don't like the look of it.

Base. (distort) Attention, everybody! Attention! Base calling. Listen, I have just picked up a message that a third member of the wrecked machine had been picked up at NP8.

Leader. M.O. here. All right men, let's get down. We'll have to start again round the other side of this mountain. Quick as you can. There must be a man still in that aircraft.

Narrator. The men clambered down and hurried to the jeep which acted as tender to the ambulance. In this they bumped and skidded over 30 miles as they skirted the base of the massive peak to attack it from another side. The jeep slithered over crumbling shale and narrow (sheep) tracks, and edged past large boulders till it could go no farther. Then, at 3 o'clock in the afternoon the search began all over again from a new base. The party had the whole of the formidable Mellyn Llyn peak (ii) to search, and daylight would soon be gone.

Leader. Now be careful you don't lose touch with one another. We haven't got any aircraft overhead to help us this time, and this peak is full of dangerous gullies. Now, the first party had better start the ascent from here see it on the map? We shan't have any visual contact. The weather is so bad now that we shall have to depend on radio.

FX. X/F Music and Off.

Narrator. But even the use of radio presented special difficulties in this wild mountain country. The range of the walky talky was only a few miles and, under certain conditions, a shelf of rock could screen a radio so completely that it would not be able to pick up base. The men had constantly to check their radios as they climbed.

FX. F/U Music and Wind.

Jimmy. Jimmy here. I'm about a thousand feet up now. I'm Just going to pull myself up to the spine of this ridge.

Orderly. (distort) I'm at the other ridge on the lee side. Footholds are very bad. Can't make very quick progress.

FX. F/O FX.

Narrator. The snow was now driving hard at them, and every now and then the men would be completely blinded by dense masses of cloud which enveloped them. Still, struggled up to two thousand feet, searching every likely spot, and then pushed up still higher, converging towards each other as they neared the very peak of the mountain. More than ever now they had to be careful to keep in touch, for this was the stiffest part of the ascent where it would be fatally easy to get lost. They were three thousand feet up when they had the first glimmer of hope.

FX. F/U Music and Wind.

Jimmy. I think I can see something. It's only a speck, but it looks....yes, I think it's an aircraft. This snow is right in my eyes... wait a minute fellers.....it's on shelf right above where you are Joe - Yes, it's an aircraft. (excited) It's an aircraft.

Leader. Listen everybody. M.O. here. Everybody concentrate on that ridge. Are you all clear which one it is?

Voices. (distorted & fainter) Yes, Yes, I'm clear.

Leader. We shall have to move like blazes. This mist is going to shut everything down very soon and the light won't last much longer.

Narrator. As daylight was fading the first members of the search party reached the wrecked machine. It loomed up out of the dripping mist, a mass of twisted metal. But inside was a man.

FX. F/U Music and Wind.

Leader. He's still breathing. Got the blankets? Poor devil... (almost to himself) exposure of course. No wonder... he's been up here over thirty hours (iii) in this muck... concussion...that looks like a fractured foot. Orderly, mind that foot as you put him on the stretcher. We've got to get him out of this double quick.

Orderly. It won't be a piece of cake getting him down sir. About fifteen hundred feet to the ambulance, I reckon.

Leader. Let's get started. Hullo base. We have found a survivor. We are starting down now. Mind you have something hot waiting....(Fade)

F/O FX.

Narrator. The injured man was strapped onto the stretcher, and the party slowly edged themselves slowly down the mountain. It was now snowing hard, and cloud enveloped the whole mountain as they made the slow, dangerous descent. A few hours later, Flying Control, waiting anxiously for news, heard a message from the ambulance.

Base. Unit has descended safely, with injured man. Hospital case. Proceeding right away.

Narrator. Thanks to the Mountain Rescue Service, that injured airman is now recovering, and will soon be flying again.

FX. Up Lillibulero – Peak and Out.

END

Author's Notes.

(i) 8 men.
(ii) Actually the Carneddau Range above Melynllyn.
(iii) In fact the period was 43 hours before rescue.

This broadcast must have been a shot in the arm for those early team members, who would walk a little taller after this wider recognition. The story chosen was a classic wartime morale booster. Sadly, and unknown to the audience of the time, most of the searches had more tragic conclusions.

Remote snow covered Foel Grach, mid left.

F/Lt. Graham leads the Llandwrog team up the hill. Note aerials on pack radios.
Caernarfon Airport Museum

Chapter Thirteen

Into Top Gear

On 3rd January 1944 came a bombshell, Flight Lieutenant Graham was posted to take over as medical officer of an RAF squadron in India. However, he left his brainchild in good hands, and on 22nd January the Air Ministry announced the official formation of the RAF Mountain Rescue Service. This to search for and rescue airmen who had crashed in mountainous areas within a radius of 40 miles of RAF stations Llandwrog for Snowdonia, Millom for the Lake District, and Wigtown for southwest Scotland.

This month was the watershed in the history of the Service. The prominence given by the Press in November had a beneficial spin off. The Air Ministry received requests from several RAF personnel with climbing experience who wished to combine a little adventure with their ground duties, and to save a few lives into the bargain. In that month then, new faces started to appear at Llandwrog. No sooner had they been found accommodation than they were presenting themselves at the Sick Bay, the headquarters of the MRU, full of anticipation for the job ahead, even before reporting to their various ground duty posts.

Sergeant Gordon Leigh was an instructor at No.1 Signals School at Cranwell when he heard of the MRS. He had been a keen hill walker and climber in the Pennines and Lake District since his youth, and was welcomed with open arms. He was a bit put out at the lack of good climbing boots, but was able to advise the team on obtaining special metal plates, known as Brigham Peacock's, for fitting to boots. These were manufactured by this Manchester firm with threaded holes, into which were screwed renewable steel studs for grip on rock or ice. These were an improvement on the boots hobnailed at the sides, and the plates were soon adopted by the team (see photo on page 74.)

Other arrivals at this time were LAC J. C. (Campy) Barrows, with extensive experience of the Pennines. He looks like he was born wearing hiking boots, and uncomfortable without them. Flying Officer John Lloyd, a medical officer with climbing experience also joined the team, to share the workload with Scudamore, as the latter had with Graham.

With the personnel came an official available issue of equipment for a team members, consisting of the following items:

Boots: ankle, grooved heel (nailed with hobs), or Boots, heavy greased.
Socks: wool blue/grey.
Frocks: white.
Smock/Trousers: windproof.
Battle-dress: serge.
Coats: duffle white.
Helmets: balaclava.
Mittens: long wool.
Stockings: seaboot.
Rucksack: Bergen
Carriers: Everest Mk III

Not all these items were available immediately, and a stretcher suitable for mountain terrain would not be provided for some years.

On the day in January that Graham was posted, Flight Lieutenant Simkins, a signals officer from Farnborough visited Llandwrog. He discussed possible locations for placing mountain warning radio beacons on approaches to the airfield. With the help of the MR team, over the next two days he

Gordon Leigh returns to his old stamping ground. Seen here by the wreck of the Boston on Carnedd Davydd with daughter Joan, son Alan and local farm friend Leon.

LAC Barrows and Flying Officer Lloyd with pack radio. See note on boots in text.
Gordon Leigh

placed one 'balloon squeaker' on the summit of Foel Grach (3195 feet), and the other on Craig Cwm Silyn (2408 feet). These continuously radiated a bleeping signal on the listening out frequency of aircraft radios, and were used extensively on barrage balloons above our cities to alert our aircraft to their presence. They had to be serviced once a week in all weathers, with new dry HT batteries, and charged accumulators. The Jeep was taken by the MRU driver and a technician, along with either team members or a couple of hefty lads from general duties to hump the heavy accumulators on a frame rucksack. For bad weather a pair of heavy duty telephone wires were laid from the squeakers down to where the Jeep ran out of track. On Foel Grach this was from the summit down to Melynllyn. In snow these wires were picked up at the bottom and traced by pulling out of the snow until the top was reached. In spite of the squeaker provision there was no immediate dramatic reduction in crashes.

The Cowlyd Anson

While most of the MRS story is told through the men who strove to save lives, the opportunity is taken to include the first hand account of one survivor recently traced. Sergeant Bob Birch trained on Harvards in Canada, hoping to be a fighter pilot but, because he was so tall at 6ft 1in with long legs, he found himself converting to twin engined aircraft and posted to RAF Cark on Morecambe Bay. This was the home of the Staff Pilot Training Unit, to provide pilots for service at Observer Advanced Flying Units. He recalls 'The important part of the course was, naturally, the flying, three day trips as pilot, and three as navigator, followed by three night trips as pilot, and three as navigator. By the end of the course's allotted time bad weather curtailed training. I had completed the day trips, but only one night trip as pilot, and none as navigator. It was decided that we would do one more night trip and declare the course finished. With typical Training Command logic, little account was taken of the weather, a cloud base of 1,500 feet, nor my total inexperience of navigating at night.

The exercise was the usual three legged trip, with the first turning point off Anglesey, in Anson LT433. We calculated the first course at briefing using the wind speed and direction as provided by the met boys, and off we went. The pilot was Sergeant Jock Grant, a pupil like myself. The pupil wireless opera-

tor was Pilot Officer M. Byrne, an Australian, and the staff W/OP was Warrant Officer Renton. The latter should have been sitting beside his pupil, but he chose instead to sit beside the pilot in the right hand seat. From a back bearing to Cark I saw that we were to port of our track. I needed three fixes (bearings) to calculate my exact position, decide where we would be in six minutes time, and give a change of course. The weather was not good and all I could see flying below cloud was the Great Bar lightship, which I used for a two line fix, calculated my change of course and passed the paper to the pilot. You always think that crashes happen to other people, but the next thing I remember clearly was waking up in the early morning on a Welsh hillside thinking 'It's happened to me!' (This was on the summit of the ridge to the west of Llyn Cowlyd, near Clogwyn Du). When I was able to take stock of the situation, I realised that poor Jock Grant had taken the brunt of the impact on the port side and was dead. P/O Byrne had a broken femur, and could not move. W/O Renton was sitting outside with his back to the nose of the aeroplane, and I could not persuade him to crawl inside. He was talking incoherently. It was snowing, but he had on an Irvin suit, so I had to leave him there. My forearm was broken in two places, as was my fibula and my ankle, all on the right side. Also I later discovered, I

'Hank the Yank'. US Army reporter Saul Levitt on MRS exercise. *Gordon Leigh*

Cpl McTigue with radio, and mountaineering instructor Sgt Hans Pick watch F/Lt Scudamore's techniques. *Gordon Leigh*

had two black eyes. The impact had torn off the wings, which were left some fifty yards behind. The fuselage had travelled on, but the front port side was crushed. At about 11 am I heard the noise of aircraft engines, and struggled out of the wreckage clutching the small dinghy Very pistol. I was just in time to see a flight of Ansons disappearing into the snow clouds. In disgust I fired the Very pistol and returned inside. Byrne and I found a parachute which we wrapped around us and helped ourselves to glucose sweets from the dinghy pack. When I next looked out I saw the wings burning. One explanation may be that the Very cartridge landed on them. Around noon a dark haired lad appeared. I took him to be a hiker (Actually Will Roberts, son of a local farmer). He obviously alerted the RAF for a few hours later the Mountain Rescue chaps from Llandwrog arrived. I think there were eight of them. They included a doctor who administered morphine all round. W/O Renton, who was later found to have a broken skull, was taken off first, then P/O Byrne, then me at 8 pm, and finally, poor old Jock. They must have been a wonderful team, the MRS boys. They grumbled good naturedly about my weight, but carried me safely and without too much discomfort down the mountainside. I think it took six of them for the stretcher because the going was rough and it was dark. A much belated

Hill walker contemplates the remains of Anson AX583 on Drum.

Humber ambulance with improved tent. Tal-y-Fan to the south. *Gordon Leigh*

'Thank You' to them, also to the nurses at Llandudno General Hospital, who were very friendly, and produced chips and Ovaltine at midnight'.

The Llandwrog team, led by Flight Lieutenant Scudamore had picked up PC William Jones at Tyn-y-Groes as guide, but had taken the track up past Llyn Eigiau to make base camp at Hafod-y-rhiw, a lake keepers cottage, instead of the nearer route to the crash up by Llyn Cowlyd. This required a long journey over the top of a boggy ridge to the Anson which was reached at 1345 hours. It was no wonder that the MR team members were running out of steam when carrying Bob Birch across the ridge and down the steep slopes, being the third in line.

Training

A Royal Artillery Officer, serving at the Air Ministry, Major C.R. Roxburgh was now given the task of overseeing the organisation of the new Service, and coordinating the policy of the various teams. Next, Sergeant Hans Pick, on loan from the 52nd Austrian Mountain Division, was appointed Air Ministry Instructor in mountain rescue. He was an ex-police officer from Vienna, and had been on many mountain rescues in the Alps. On 4th April he arrived at Llandwrog and gave the team members a 14 day course in map and compass navigation, rock climbing, and casualty evacuation. While some of the existing members may already have been competent in these skills, at least the training at all MRS bases would be standardised, and Sergeant Pick would take some strain off the associated medical officers.

On 12th April 1944 Sergeant Saul Levitt, of the US Army, and staff correspondent of the magazine 'Yank', arrived to spend some time with the team and write an article on it. He had been until recently the radio operator on an operational B-17 Fortress, but due to an accident in a Jeep, had been transferred to 'Yank' because he was a pre-war journalist. He came at a time of a temporary lull in incidents, but as Sergeant Pick was treating the team to cross country training exercises. In these, members would be dropped off from a truck at intervals and have to find their way to a reference point on the map carried, with the aid of a ruler, protractor, and compass. Of men and mountains on a training run Levitt observed 'We parked the truck and pitched the tent above a lake. A farmer's little kids couldn't speak any English, hid behind their mother's back and watched the soldiers (team) out of big eyes. We offered them something to eat, which kids understand in all languages. Jock, who has the makings of a GI big operator, worked out a deal whereby

The Llandwrog team on a map exercise with Sergeant Hans Pick. *Gordon Leigh*

the shepherd's wife gave us four eggs and a quart of fresh milk for some of the tinned stuff that we carried in the truck.

The originals at the base in Wales have still the most accomplished record of life saving of all. The rules are simple, you never stop looking, and they have looked for as long as four days at a time. In over two years they have never failed to find any crashed plane, to bring the living to recovery, and the dead to the decency of burial. They have worked through nights, signalling to each other through the 'screen' of valleys, which separate one man from another, with Very flares. Their spiked shoes have ploughed through marshland and dug into slippery inclines....These are gaunt old mountains, with the topsoil thinned out and the worn rock face showing. The height of the highest peak, 3,600 ft. shouldn't start you sneering, even if you're from Colorado, for this is lonely rugged country, inhabited here and there by shepherds, with lots of sheer rock face, tumbling mountain streams, and razor edge ridges that are too tough even for the nimble footed hungry sheep. Winter, the parade of weather is all on the villainous side, fog, mist, dampness, and often a powdery blowing snow that drives through the valleys as if under the horsepower kick of a snowplough'. After the war Saul Levitt would resume his New York writing career, with 'The Sun is Silent', a fine novel about the USAAF, and a Broadway play 'The Andersonville Trial' earned an Emmy award when produced on television.

The crashes still carried on, month in month out. On 25th April 1944, RAF Millom, on the Cumbrian coast, notified Llandwrog that they had lost Anson AX583, on a course of 200 degrees towards Conway, and it was presumed down in the mountains. The message was passed to the MR Unit at 0430 hours. After considering the likely area for the loss, Flight Lieutenant Scudamore and the MR team left and searched Foel Fras and Foel Grach. At 1245 hours a message was passed to the Humber ambulance at Melynllyn that the Anson had been found by an Army patrol on manoeuvres near the summit of 2,529 feet Drum. When the team arrived, following a drive to Bwlch y Ddeufaen, and another strenuous climb, the Anson was found pointing 5 degrees off course. The crew of five had all been killed outright. Gordon Leigh recalls 'We had to cut pieces out of the aircraft, and use ropes to pull it apart to bring the crew out. We got the last body down about 8 pm and strapped them onto stretchers in a 15 cwt truck, two each side and the fifth on his side in between the others. We had been out all day without a meal and a stop was made at a pub in Conway where we were able to have a drink and a sandwich. In the middle of this there was such a commotion and screaming outside that we all dashed out to see what was the matter. A nosy woman had seen the truck with the canvas back and decided to undo the straps and peep inside with a torch which everyone carried in wartime during the blackout. When she shone it inside she came face to face with a dead airman and promptly passed out on the spot!'

Sergeant Bob Birch, survivor from Anson LT443, far right, at 37 SFTS Calgary.

Chapter Fourteen

Never a Quiet Moment

One might assume that by 1944, the location of Snowdonia was firmly imprinted in the minds of all aircrew in the UK, but the collisions with these mountains continued at a high level throughout the year. The problem may have been that there were often many aircraft losses almost every day from bomber airfields to the east, and the odd one in the mountains by an aircraft which had overshot its airfield returning from operations, or on a training flight, would not have been of great note except to friends and relatives of those concerned. At Llandwrog, and the other north Wales airfields, there was pressure for flying to continue apace, especially to replace the high losses in Bomber Command, and trainee navigators and others still made errors through inexperience. Mainly it was the weather, which was rarely trustworthy, and meteorological forecasting had not reached the satellite art of today, which is still far from exact. When team members were not engaged with crashes, they would be training on the hills, or carrying out their regular vital work at the airfield.

Even so, it was not all always the mountains which gave trouble. In the early hours of 1st June, Anson MG340 overshot the runway during a thunderstorm, and plunged into the sea about one mile offshore. The medical officer, Tom Scudamore was called from his bed: 'All the mountain rescue team went down to the beach and shone a searchlight around, but could see nothing. The officer in charge of flying control turned in, saying there was nothing they could do. I went over to the nearest Anson on the airfield, tore a dinghy out, and asked for volunteers while we inflated it. The dinghy was dragged to the sea and launched by the light of the headlights of the MRU vehicles. Four rescuers headed out to where Very lights had been seen. What amazed me was the luminescent plankton on the surface of the water. After paddling for half an hour we saw Very lights, not from the aircraft, but from a dinghy. We saw several figures lit by the frequent lightning. We were informed that all five survivors were safe, the dinghy drill having gone without a hitch. We tied the two dinghies together and paddled towards the shore. We could now see numerous bright lights and masses of people, reminiscent of Blackpool. While the dinghies were still some distance from the shore, we could see two figures in the water swimming towards us. This was a brave gesture, for they must have been deadbeat. They were hauled aboard, and recognised as Flying Officer H.King, appropriately the Air/Sea rescue officer, and Corporal Ernie Jackson, of the MR team. On reaching the shore all the party proceeded to Station Sick Quarters, where the wet clothes were discarded in the warm operating theatre, and all admitted to the ward for the night with an issue of rum followed by hot tea'. For his pains, Flight Lieutenant Scudamore received an admonishment next morning from the O.C. Flying for removing the dinghy from the Anson, thus immobilising it from flying that day!

The mountain crashes continued, unabated. On 8th June Anson LT116 from Llandwrog was posted overdue, and a farmer at Ty Gwyn Farm in Nant Ffrancon reported he had heard a low flying aircraft, followed by a flash and thud soon afterwards high above on Mynydd Perfedd. Called from their beds at 0445 hours, the team left half an hour later, taking with them two instructors,

Mynydd Perfedd, last resting place of Ansons LT116 and LT184, high above Maes Caradoc Farm from which the Llandwrog MR Team climbed in atrocious weather.

Remains of Anson LT116 below the cliffs of Mynydd Perfedd. Undercarriage assembly and wheel.

Wireless operator Sergeant L. J. Pearce, who lost his life in Anson LT116 on the 8th June 1944. *Mrs P. Hughes (daughter)*

whose pupil wireless operators, Sergeant L.J.Pearce (married to a local girl), and an Australian were on board. The rest of the crew comprised an Australian pilot and navigator, and a Canadian air bomber. The Anson was found 300 feet below the summit. All the crew had been killed outright and had to be extricated and brought down from a perilous position. The two instructors were most distressed at finding their charges like this, and aircrew did not go out with the team again.

Civilian Rescues

Another area of incidents which reared its head at this time was involvement with civilian rescues, still continuing today. At 0130 hours on 16th June 1944 a call came in from the Dolgelly police that a girl climber was stuck on the cliffs of Cader Idris. As this was a great distance from Llandwrog, Flying Officer Lloyd and Corporal McTigue raced to Dolgelly in the Jeep, leaving the Humber ambulance for any other emergency. Arriving eventually at Dyfryddan Farm, with a policeman, they were led up to the cliff by the farmer, who was uncertain where the girl had been seen. Lloyd and McTigue scaled the cliff via a gully, and scanned the cliff face, but to no avail. On descending to the cliff base, another farmer, who had observed the girl, led them to towards a ledge high up off another gully. This could not be reached direct, so Lloyd managed to climb down from above, while McTigue approached from another direction, only to find that the there was no one on the ledge. All this effort was expended in driving rain and a bitter wind. On returning to the farm, they found the missing girl, who had managed to pull herself together, and climb up the rock face above the ledge and thence to safety. This was the first time that the MRS had gone out to rescue a civilian and the reasons setting this precedent, recorded by F/O John Lloyd, are significant since, though the primary task of the MRS was to save downed aircrew in the mountains, from the end of the war the majority of searches would involve civilians.

'(1) There is little doubt that the MRS has the most efficient equipment and is the best organisation for dealing with mountain casualties of all sorts within a radius of 40 miles of this station.

'(2) The police in this neighbourhood are of the utmost value to us in locating aircraft crashes and it is felt that our present relations with them would deteriorate if we refused to help them with civilian accidents, which are primarily their responsibility'.

It is true that many policemen across Snowdonia were a great help. Not only did they collate information on any unusual sounds or sights of explosions in the mountains, which might have been associated with aircraft, they knew their own patches intimately, even high ground. One of these was William Jones, PC99 of the Caernarvonshire Constabulary, who was usually picked up from Tyn-y-Groes police station as a guide when the team approached the Carneddau range from the Conway valley. His knowledge of the area and stamina are legendary. His nickname was 'Champion', from his prowess in boxing. It also suited his prowess on the hills. He was one of several policemen who aided the team at times.

The Llandwrog team were again involved with civilians soon afterwards. On 1st August, Corporal Jackson and LAC Barrows were taking signals personnel to service the radio squeaker on Foel Grach through an Army Practice Gunnery Range. Campy Barrows relates 'At the foot of the mountain track Army spotters signalled the gunners to stop firing so we could carry out our duties. At 1.00 pm, as the track to Melynllyn ran out onto the open moor we were stopped by an Army officer, asking could we help at an accident? Higher up the track we found a group of hikers, three of whom had been seriously hurt by mortar fire. They were a Christian Holidays Association group walking from Llanfairfechan, over Drum, to the Conway valley. They saw mortars bursting up the valley, and were cutting across to avoid them when, without warning the gunners altered range. Those badly injured were a young girl who had been hit in the breast, a man with his left arm almost severed, and a man with shrapnel in his chest. Emergency first-aid was given, with a wire used as a tourniquet for the arm as the victim was losing a great deal of blood, and bandages applied to stop blood loss in the other cases. Two cases were taken down to Tal-y-Bont by Army lorry, with the third in the Jeep, a nightmare journey for the injured along the bumpy track. 'The hospital records do not survive, but is is believed that the girl lost a breast, and the man's arm was amputated. The other victim is thought to have died later through a punctured lung. The team however still had to return up the track to climb Foel Grach, having made sure there was to be no more shelling that day. Future visits would always be made with some anxiety.

Moel Hebog, scene of the last mountain crash from Llandwrog, 13th June 1944. The MR Team rescued Sergeant Harry Howard, the sole survivor. *Gordon Leigh*

The Llandwrog MR Team leaps into action on a call out. Note spotlights, shaded headlights being almost useless. *Caernarfon Airport Museum*

Chapter Fifteen

The Llandwrog Mountain Rescue Team Members

This happy band of volunteers were special men. Without their dedication, many of the survivors they rescued would most likely have perished. They did not seek praise, only to do their work quietly on the mountains they grew to love, though with great respect for potential dangers. Their fine example would be emulated by the other RAF teams set up elsewhere.

It is time to say a little of what we know of the Llandwrog team members. The list is not exhaustive, and may not include all the volunteers or those who were not with the team for very long. The writer's apologies for any so missed; their combined team efforts are what matter. The founding members of Flight Lieutenant Graham's initial team in 1942 were: Nursing Orderly Corporal Gregory McTigue from Merseyside. His stalwart contribution was recognised by the award of the British Empire Medal in the New Year Honours list in 1945. He married a WAAF (Eunice) an auxiliary nurse in the Sick Bay at Llandwrog, and went into nursing after the war and it is sad to relate he lost his life in a road accident in 1978, a few days before the writer traced his address in the hope of obtaining his wartime experiences.

Another nursing orderly, Corporal Ernie Jackson, was a civilian ambulance driver in London during the Blitz, and had then served in the RAF in the Middle East before arriving at Llandwrog. Sergeant Bill Harvey was the senior NCO in the Sick Bay, and ran it while the medical officers were on the mountains, though on occasions he was known to have \been on the searches himself.

Corporal Reg Martin was in charge of MT (Motor Transport) for the team, and often drove the four wheel drive Humber ambulance, with LAC Tommy (Jock) Cummings driving the Jeep, unless Graham chose to. Both changed gear into the search and rescue role on arrival in the mountains. Corporal Sid Baker was the invaluable wireless operator in the ambulance, keeping in touch with the team members out on the hills with their short range radios, and base at Llandwrog by long range W/T (Wireless Telegraphy). Flying Officer Tom Scudamore was an important bridge in the team from his gradual involvement in May 1943, and was already versed in George Graham's ways and dedication, when he took over as Station Medical Officer when Graham departed in January 1944. About the same time two other founder members were posted, Reg Martin going to 151 Recovery Unit at Odiham to prepare for the invasion, and Ernie Jackson to India.

The new blood early in 1944, some already mentioned, included Flying Officer John Lloyd, Sergeant Gordon Leigh, LAC Campy Barrows, Corporal Moe Chuwen, a Physical Training and Parachute Jump Instructor. Other known members were LAC's Jim Bradford, often driver of the Humber ambulance, Johnny D'eath, Jock Howie, sometime Jeep driver, and Freddie McLune. A fortunate posting brought a local man, T.A.Williams, here in May 1944, after service abroad. He had an intimate knowledge of the uplands area and was able to advise the team of the cart tracks and paths available for rapid approaches to the hills that they did not already know.

Flight Lieutenant George Desmond Graham. D.S.O. M.B.E.

This officer was born at Carlisle on 20th March 1913, and qualified as a doctor at St.

Bartholemew's Hospital in September 1939. In the meantime he had become a member of the hospital's Climbing Club, with experience in the Swiss Alps, presumably following climbing his native Lakeland fells. After working at the London Fever Hospital, he joined the RAF in February 1941 as a Flying Officer, service No.61855. By one of those strokes of good fortune he was posted to RAF Llandwrog as Station Medical Officer, with the rank of Flight Lieutenant. When one looks back on the origins of the RAF Mountain Rescue Service, the question arises as to what qualities this medical officer possessed in foresight, leadership, and dealing with that autocratic machine known as the Air Ministry from his comparatively junior rank. Tom Scudamore reveals something of the man for us. 'Dr Graham was a tall slim gentleman, with very thin straight hair, a large fair bristling moustache, and a powerful voice. He was a man who knew where he was going and what he wanted. On my first visit to a crash I was told to get in the Jeep with Graham. It was a big mistake; you should have seen him driving to a crash. I do so object to cutting ALL the corners!'

Graham had been writing to the Air Ministry since mid 1942 when he realised there were no facilities whatsoever for organising search and rescue parties in the mountains. So he wrote to Group, and Flying Training Command, and they passed the letters on to Air Ministry. Next he would receive an admonishment from the Station Commander, Group Captain G. W. Bentley, who advised him in no uncertain terms of the correct procedure. This did not deter Graham, who persisted by writing direct to the Air Ministry. This unorthodox approach eventually produced the desired effect in that a medical officer, Wing Commander Ruffel Smith, who was also a pilot, was despatched from the Air Ministry to look into Graham's requests for equipment which eventually resulted in his redesigned team of July 1943. Graham's dedication to saving life was unequalled even off the hills. When notified of the crash of Anson LV152 into the sea near Trevor on 9th September 1943, he raced along the coast with team members to find that three survivors had been brought ashore. While giving them first aid he was told that three others were still in the Anson. He immediately swam out and gave the Air Sea Rescue crew a hand to cut a hole in the side of the aircraft and succeeded in extricating a crew member and an Air Training Corps cadet. He gave the two young men artificial respiration until he reluctantly had to admit defeat.

Staff pilot George Bates; 'It was an inspiration to know him. His efforts raised the morale amongst aircrew by comforting them with the feeling that if they survived a crash in the mountains, a dedicated and skilled med-

Original pre-1944 Llandwrog MR Team. Left to right: LAC Jackson, Cpl McTigue, F/Lt Graham, F/Lt Scudamore, Sgt Harvey, LAC Martin, nursing orderly. *Tom Scudamore*

Early MR Team with support staff. *Mrs McTigue*

Radio operator Corporal Sid Baker in the Humber ambulance. *Reg Martin*

Flight Lieutenant Tom Scudamore with team members and support staff in 1944. *Dr T. O. Scudamore*

ical team would come to their aid, regardless of the difficulties.' After his posting to India, two stories filtered back, the first via Tom Scudamore who tells us that Graham was sharing a room with a dentist who observed 'I've got this extraordinary man sharing rooms with me, Dr Graham, who has just arrived from north Wales. To go to the Officers Mess he wears this nice RAF officer's tunic, and neat collar and tie. But when you look closely, he has a pair of airman's battledress trousers with no crease, which are held up by a piece of mountain rope, and from this dangles a large Scout knife!' One can only imagine this impact on his fellow officers, who were imbued into setting an example of rank and class of the British Officer abroad. Their view of him would soon be greatly modified.

Into Burma

If Flight Lieutenant Graham thought that he had bade goodbye to the mountains he was wrong. He had been posted as medical officer to No.357 Squadron at Dum Dum. Another unit, No.1576 Special Duties Flight operated Lockheed Hudsons for dropping agents and supplies to resistance teams in Japanese held territory. On the evening of 14th March 1944, Hudson AM949 (A) failed to return from a sortie to drop supplies at Bhamo, near Kohang on the Burma/Siam border. Many hours later an agent radioed that the Hudson had hit the top of a 6,000 feet mountain and four of the crew had been killed, but two were still alive and required immediate medical help. When Graham heard of this he straight away volunteered to parachute in to the survivors, though he had no experience or training. Permission was granted and Flight Sergeant T. E. (Chalky) White, a parachute instructor, volunteered to accompany him. After giving Graham basic briefing on how to leave the aircraft and control his descent, their Hudson took off at 2350 hours on the 16th from Dum Dum, near Calcutta, refuelling at Chittagong. They arrived at the Drop Zone at dawn, and dropped containers of medical and other supplies. Next time round the red light came on and White shouted 'Action Stations' into Graham's ear, followed by 'Go' on the green. They left the Hudson close together so that White could shout instructions on their short descent. Graham just missed a tree and did a rugby roll on landing, sustaining nothing worse than a bang on the head.

A group of natives guided them four miles along narrow jungle trails to the crash site, where the local agent, Major Leach, had set up base in a cattle hut for the casualties.

Unfortunately one survivor, Flight Lieutenant Ponsford, had died after guarding his comrade with a drawn revolver, and only Flying Officer Wally P.Prosser, the Canadian navigator remained alive. He and Ponsford had finished their tour but had accompanied the crew of the Hudson since they were familiar with the area. A local witch doctor had covered Prosser's head wound, a fractured skull, with a filthy mess of herbs. This had to be gently cleaned off before treatment, then a fractured right ankle dealt with by a plaster cast from toes to knee. Turns were taken so that the casualty was watched through the night, but Prosser was weaker next day. However, Captain Ankins, a US Army doctor, who had made a long mule trip from the Chinese border, arrived and helped Graham to devise a nasal drip for some special food brought along, with tubing from the wreck.

Prosser hovered between life and death for the next few days when there came news that the Japanese and Burmese Puppet Troops were attempting to enter the area. Major Leach advised evacuation before all the road links were severed. A litter was constructed for the patient, and two days later, on 30th March, the Japanese troops were observed moving up the valley. Graham's party, including sturdy litter bearers slipped away just in time in torrential rain. Over the next few days progress was made over difficult terrain to the US Army doctor's outpost, stopping in village huts at night. At the border their guerrilla friends left, in case they were commandeered by the Chinese Army. The Chinese Colonel was supposed to provide enough coolies to complete the journey, but only supplied eight, and these to climb the highest mountain en route. Also the Chinese

Flight Lieutenant George Graham, MBE in reflective mood. *Daily Express*

refused permission to clear a landing strip to fly Prosser out, which would add another five days to the journey. The only cheer in all this was that Prosser gained consciousness at that time. The coolies proved to be uncooperative, but by dint of persuasion by Graham's Colt revolver, they reached their objective for the night. This must rank as one of the few occasions in history where a doctor used a gun to save a life!

Next morning the coolies had deserted, and only four deplorable replacements could be found. Tom White went ahead with the mules to obtain help from the next US Army outpost. On retracing his steps, Graham and his party could not be found so White returned to the outpost. In the early hours of the next morning Graham was heard calling 'Chalky' at the top of his voice. He had struggled through the dense jungle trails, and crossed two rivers with the four coolies and Prosser, topping the natives up with rum to keep them going. He left the track to persuade some men from a village to finish the journey. Another day on, some twenty miles were covered, and by now Prosser was becoming stronger. But the last day on foot was the hardest, again through the mountains, at times in the sweltering heat of the valleys, and a few hours later suffering freezing hailstorms on the peaks until they preached Shunning, a US base.

Eventually on 17th April, they flew in a Curtiss Commando from Yunnanni Airport, over the 'Hump' at 20,000 feet to Assam, changing to a Dakota for the last leg. Flying Officer Prosser was delivered to the British General Hospital at Calcutta and made a good recovery. For this courageous effort Flight Lieutenant Graham was awarded an immediate Distinguished Service Order, and Flight Sergeant White the Conspicuous Gallantry Medal (Flying).

George Graham had again been in the right place at the right time. It is sad to relate that this gallant, caring, gentleman contracted ill health while serving in India and Burma. We know little of his life from then on, except that he may have practised in Northampton for some years. He died at the Royal Cheadle Hospital, 19th October 1980.

Flight Sergeant T. E. White, CGM (Flying) *Reg Martin*

Wally Prosser in the uniform of the Southern Alberta Regiment, before transferring to the RCAF. *via Charles Birch*

Chapter Sixteen

The End of the Beginning

The ushering in of the year 1945 finally found a reduction, though not cessation, in the number of mountain crashes in Snowdonia. The wartime Anson losses to these mountains had been conquered but, from September 1944 to the time the team left Llandwrog, they saved not one more life. This was not the fault of the team. Following the Anson crashes, where there were often successes, due to the relatively slow speed of the aircraft, the rest were not survivable. There were still the searches and climbs to recover the aircrew involved. From its inception in July 1942 to June 1945 the team were involved in one way or another with 58 aircraft crashes, from which 73 airmen were saved. Of these, A few made their own way down mountains to raise the alarm, and some were helped by civilians or police. Nearly all were treated by the team's medical officer and orderlies before evacuation to hospital or Station Sick Quarters.

The last crash over 3,000 feet dealt with by the Llandwrog Team was in February. A USAAF Martin B-26 Marauder medium bomber serial 44-68072, with a crew of five, had taken the southern route across the Atlantic and eventually arrived at RAF St.Mawgan in Cornwall. At 1238 hours on 1st February the aircraft took off for delivery to Burtonwood, near Warrington. It never arrived. At 1445 hours next day, the team was notified by Flying Control that the aircraft was missing and added that a Crosville bus driver had reported that the previous day, while in Nant Peris, at the bottom of Llanberis Pass, he had heard an aircraft circling around low in cloud, followed by a deafening crash from the mountains over towards Bethesda. The MR team, led by Flight Lieutenant Tom Scudamore, was away by 1600 hours, setting up a mountain HQ in the Humber ambulance at Fron Rhedyn in Nant Peris an hour later. Leaving a radio operator there, three teams of two men set out in approaching darkness, one to search 3,030 feet Elidir Fawr, another for Foel Goch, and a third crossed the Afon Gafr to ascend 3,104 feet Y Garn. With HQ at around 500 feet, each party had a gruelling, unremitting, climb in store.

Campy Barrows: 'The Dental Officer and self headed for the south ridge from Cwm Creifio, crossing over ground boggy after a recent thaw, and streams in spate until we hit the ridge above the Devil's Kitchen, where we turned for the summit. The weather changed to a cold wind and mist and, at one time we were caught in a vicious hailstorm lasting ten minutes. On reaching the summit we made a call to base, and heard that at 1845 hours the second party had found some aircraft and human remains at the edge of a precipice leading south to the summit of Y Garn. In view of this outcome, with no possibility of survivors, the weather, and the danger of the location, the teams made for base. On descending we were given a welcome cup of tea at Gwastadnant Farm. On returning to the Humber I got the Primus stove going to cook some sausages. Just as I was lifting them into the pan a sheepdog appeared from nowhere and spirited away several links. We found it quite hilarious to see the sheepdog disappearing into the gloom with the links of sausage trailing along, a little light relief in the midst of a tragedy. We got to bed at 2 a.m.'

They were out again next morning and up to the crash site by 1215 hours. The Marauder, which had been blown by unpredicted

Double Wasp radial engine from B-26 Marauder 44-68072.

3030ft Y Garn, middle left. *Gordon Leigh*

Pathetic remains of B-17 Flying Fortress on Graig Cwm Llwyd. *Dave Roberts*

winds many miles west of its intended track, had hit the grassy slope at 3,000 feet, and fallen over the 1,000 feet precipice into Cwm Cwnion. While the body of one of the crew was found near the summit, the other four had to be recovered from the base of the cliff. They were carried on two stretchers down rough scree and steep slopes to a hut near Ogwen Cottage where they were collected along with the team members at 1830 hours. The whole party were then loaned a room to take tea and sandwiches at the Ogwen Youth Hostel before returning to Llandwrog. Of the sledge stretchers, it was recorded that one was the Duff type, and the other a converted General Service type, 'Sergeant Pick pattern': both were indispensible.

A slate plaque in memory of the Marauder crew, erected by the Snowdonia Aviation Historical Group, can be found in a lay-by in Llanberis Pass.

In between the fewer crash attendances the opportunity was now taken to hold more mountain training and navigation exercises. Tests of a special casualty bag were carried out on 1st March on Craig Cwm Silyn. It was found that a patient could be carried by six fit men each holding one of the three handles each side, but a task made easier by the insertion of wooden poles through the handles. The only problem was that there was no support for the head. The bag contained an electrical element heated by an accumulator which the team felt was an unnecessary refinement as hot water bottles were available, and the batteries were awkward and heavy to carry up mountains. However the casualty bag was considered to be a useful item and was recommended for adoption.

The last crash attended by the Llandwrog team occurred while they were transferring to RAF Llanbedr on the closure of No.9(O)AFU at Llandwrog, and involved the greatest loss of life. On 7th June 1945, Flight Lieutenant Scudamore was posted to Llanbedr in advance of the main party of the MRS. At 1430 hours the following day Flying Officer Gibson, the medical officer at Llanbedr was notified that a B-17 Flying Fortress from Polebrook on its way home to the United States via Valley, had crashed into Craig Cwm Llwyd, a western outlier of Cader Idris, opposite Barmouth. He set off for the site after advising the Llandwrog team to call at Llanbedr for directions. The aircraft was found to have collided with the northwest face of the mountain at a height of 1,200 feet, and burnt out. All that remained was the heartbreaking job to recover a total of 20 bodies from the wreckage, and transport them about a mile to the Roman Road.

The last entry in the log as a Llandwrog Team was of an unsung workhorse; 'A special mention must be made of the performance of the Jeeps. These vehicles negotiated a mountain track, almost non-existent in places, and got within 200 yards of the crash. They were invaluable in ferrying personnel and bodies between the scene of the crash and mountain HQ, which was established 1 mile away'. (Signed) T.O. Scudamore, F/Lt.

Following this entry, the North Wales team would be known as the Llanbedr Team, until its move to RAF Valley in 1949, where it has been based ever since. Standing on the airfield, the distant peaks of Snowdonia appear picturesque, inviting, and benign. Members of the RAF Mountain Rescue Service, past and present, know differently.

On 16th September 1993 the RAF Mountain Rescue Service held its 50th Anniversary at Bangor University, not very far from where it first came to life. The writer was privileged to be invited and, at dinner, sat between the only two ex-Llandwrog team members present, Campy Barrows and Moe Chuwen. As I looked around at the many faces obviously enjoying themselves with celebratory drinks at their elbows, I went back in time for a moment to those other pioneers no longer with us, to those they saved and those, in spite of heroic attempts that they were unable to.

Looking very sick! Llandwrog Sick Bay in 1978, at the time a sweet factory, now alas abandoned to the elements.

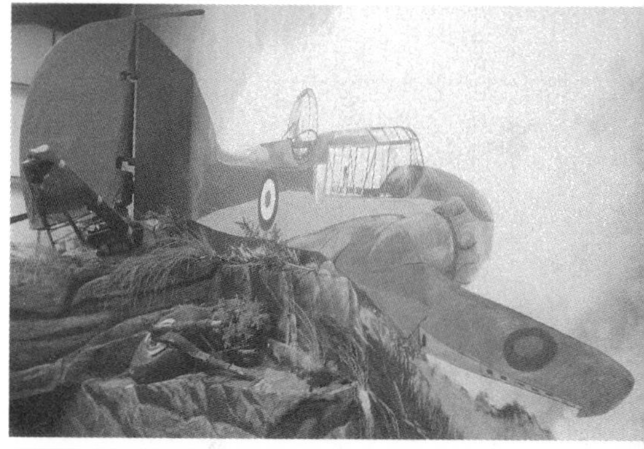

Crashed Anson display at Caernarfon Air World museum at the old airfield.
Gordon Leigh

Unsung workhorse; a Willys Jeep carrying stretcher, axe and spade, with Cpl McTigue, Cpl Jackson and LAC Cummings.
Gordon Leigh

Appendix A

RAF Llandwrog Mountain Rescue Team Crash Attendances

Date	Call Time	Aircraft	Serial	Location	Casualties
20.07.42	N/K	Botha	W5142	Moel Wnion	6S
26.07.42	..	Wellington	DV800	Black Ladders(19th)	5K
23.08.42	..	Botha	L6318	Tal-y-Fan	5K
28.09.42	..	Whitley	BD232	Llyn Dulyn(26th)	5K
19.10.42	..	Boston	Z2186	Carnedd Davydd(17th)	2K 1S
31.10.42	..	Wellington	BK234	Nr Bangor, collision	5K
31.10.42	..	Beaufighter	X7845	.. .. ..	2K
20.11.42	1200	Henley	L3334	Craig Cwm Silyn	1K
20.11.42	1500	Anson	N4981	Moel Eilio	5K
29.11.42	1400	Anson	DJ635	Foel Gron. (28th)	4K 1S (D)
22.12.42	N/K	Wellington	W5494	Gerlan, Bethesda	5K
15.01.43	1530	Anson	EG110	Foel Grach (14th)	2K 2S
04.02.43	N/K	Hudson	AM832	Llechog, Snowdon	4K
16.02.43	..	Wellington	HE466	Foel Grach (13th)	5K
01.03.43	..	Anson	EG129	Nr. Penygroes	5K
11.04.43	..	Blenheim	V6099	Elidir Fach.(30.3.43)	3K
29.04.43	..	Anson	EF823	Pencreirgiau'r Llan (28th)	5S
29.04.43	..	Anson	EF926	Nr Pant Glas	4S

Key: (D) = Died in hospital; K = Killed; S = Saved; Crash dates in brackets.

Redesigned Team Operative: Crash Log Started 6th July 1943

Date	Call Time	Aircraft	Serial	Location	Casualties
06.07.43	0745	Lancaster	R5736	Llangerniew	6K
24.07.43	1425	Oxford	W6628	Tyn-y-Groes	1S
18.08.43	2300	Ventura	AE688	Carnedd Davydd	4K
23.08.43	1030	Anson	N5371	Foel Fras	5S
29.08.43	1700	Botha	L6202	Llwydmor	4K
04.09.43	1110	Anson	EG278	Parciau, Caernarvon	4K
08.09.43	AM	Anson	EF978	Sea, near airfield	1K 4S
09.09.43	1715	Anson	LV152	Sea, near Trevor	3K 3S
05.10.43	0015	Anson	LT184	Mynydd Perfedd	4K
08.11.43	2055	Anson	N9855	Pen Yr Ole Wen	5K
20.11.43	0815	Wellington	LB185	Moel y Croesau	4K 2S
20.11.43	1230	Anson	MG111	Craig Cwm Silyn	5K
01.12.43	1230	Anson	EF909	Foel Grach (30.11.43)	4S
26.12.43	1800	Anson	EF953	Bwlch-y-Llan	4K
04.01.44	1015	Halifax	DT626	Pentre Voelas	7K
07.01.44	1345	B-24.	42-99991	Nr Llanfairfechan	5K 6S
14.01.44	2245	Anson	MG627	Nr Llanallgo, Anglesey	4S
27.01.44	2300	Wellington	HF911	Moel Fodair	3K

Date	Call Time	Aircraft	Serial	Location	Casualties
10.02.44	1745	Mosquito	LR412	Reported missing...	
14.02.44	1900	Mosquito	LR412	found on Aran Fawddwy	2K
16.02.44	1600	Anson	N5130	Nr. Llandudno Jctn	5K
21.02.44	1135	Anson	LT433	Above Llyn Cowlyd (20th)	1K 3S
29.03.44	1405	C-47	43-15105	Tremorfa, Nr. Conway	5S
25.04.44	0430	Anson	AX583	Drum	5K
16.05.44	0110	Wellington	HF519	Nr. Llanrwst	6K
01.06.44	0110	Anson	MG340	Sea, off airfield	5S
08.06.44	0445	Anson	LT116	Mynydd Perfedd	5K
13.06.44	0145	Anson	EG472	Moel Hebog	4K 1S
16.06.44	0130	First civilian		Cader Idris	
08.07.44	1115	P-47	41-6195	Nr. Aled Reservoir	1S
12.07.44	0245	Anson	MG804	Foel Fras	1K 4S
01.08.44		Injured civilians		Dulyn valley	
31.08.44	0150	Halifax	LL283	Nr. Portmadoc	2K 6S
03.09.44	1515	Halifax	JD417	Yr Eifl	6K
22.09.44	1000	P-47	41-6246	Aran Fawddwy (on 16th)	1K
25.09.44	0100	Mosquito	HX862	Drum	2K
01.11.44	2210	Mosquito	W4088	Mynydd Mawr	2K
22.11.44	1430	C-47	43-48473	Craig Dulyn (on 12th)	4K
02.02.45	1445	B-26	44-68072	Y Garn (1st)	5K
05.02.45	1645	Oxford	LB537	Llyn Crafnant (13.1.)	4K
04.04.45	0600	Anson	LT238	Near Bala	4K
17.05.45	1100	P-51	44-72340	Aran Fawddwy	1K
07.06.45	MR Team advance party transfer to RAF Llanbedr				
08.06.45	1430	B-17	44-6005	Craig Cwm Llwyd	20K

Appendix B

Bibliography

Annand, D. Wg/Cdr. *RAF Penrhos, RAF Llandwrog.* Private publication 1986.

Card, Frank. *Whensoever.* Ernest Press 1993. Comprehensive history of the RAF Mountain Rescue Service to the present day.

Doylerush, E. *No Landing Place.* Midland Counties Publications 1985. The background to aircraft crashes in Snowdonia & stories of survivors.

Doylerush, E. *Fallen Eagles.* Midland Counties Publications 1990. Similar work to above covering north-east & mid Wales. Includes story of Llandwrog Anson EF823.

Moffat, G. *Two Star Red.* Hodder & Stoughton 1964. The story of the RAF Mountain Rescue Service until 1964, told from a climber's viewpoint.

Sloan, R. *Wings of War Over Gwynedd.* Gwasg Carreg Gwalch 1991.

Smith, D.J. *Action Stations 3. Military Airfields of Wales & North West.* PSL 1981.

Smith, D.J. *Britain's Military Airfields 1939-45.* PSL 1989.

Appendix C

Log Book Extracts

Extract from Flying Log Book of staff pilot F/O Jack Stephenson.

Even in such a short space of time 6th to 19th June 1944, this log is full of interest. On the 6th and 14th Air/Sea rescue activities were carried out, the first diverting from a navigation exercise.

On 7th, 13th, and 15th the aircraft was recalled to base due to notification of bad weather coming in (code BBA).

Year 1944 Month	Date	Aircraft Type	Aircraft No.	Pilot, or 1st Pilot	2nd Pilot, Pupil or Passenger	Duty (Including Results and Remarks)
JUNE	6	ANSON	622	SELF	4 CREW	NAVIGATION diverted for A.S.R.
–	–	–	399	"	–	–
–	7	"	279	"	P/O PETCH	BEAM
–	–	–	279	P/O PETCH	SELF	–
"	–	"	622	SELF	4 CREW	NAVIGATION
"	–	"	623	"	–	– BBA
"	10	"	986	–	"	– landed at WOODVALE
"	12	"	399	"	Sgt ASHBROOK 3 Crew	"
"	13	"	222	"	4 Crew	" BBA.
"	14	"	142	"	F/Lt CLARK. F/O SPARKE HERSCOT F/S FAZACKERLEY	dinghy in Cardigan Bay Air-Sea Rescue. (not found)
"	15	"	634	"	4 Crew	NAVIGATION BBA.
"	17	"	979	"	1 "	NFT Landed at REDNAL & Montford Bridge
"	18	"	979	"	4 "	NAVIGATION
"	19	"	736	"	"	"
"	"	–	981	"	"	"

GRAND TOTAL [Cols. (1) to (10)] 809 Hrs. 20 Mins. TOTALS CARRIED FORWARD

Date 20/5/1943. Place LLANDWROG.

TIME	DETAILS OF CALLS, MESSAGES, &c.	REMARKS	TIME OF ORIGIN OF MESSAGE
	BOMBING.	SGT TRAVIS (W/OP)	
cP	ANSON 978 SGT THORNTON (PILOT)		
	IFF OK. INT/COMM OK.		
0040	ON WATCH. Davis.		
0050	AIRBORNE. IFF "ON."		
	YN9 v G2LCP 88Z - X162 X548 J/F +		
	G2LCP v YN9 R - X639 - 0055 - X100 +		
	YN9 v G2LCP R - INT C/S PENRHOS J/F +		
0120	G2LCP v YN9 QI +		
	OVER TO PENRHOS J/F +		
	A7Y v G2LCP R - X314 - AAA BOMBING.		
26	G2LCP v A7Y R +		
	A7Y v G2LCP X443 +		
0131	G2LCP v A7Y R - X445 - 0131 +		
	OVER TO YN9.		
	YN9 v G2LCP BAR +		
0147	G2LCP v YN9 R - QDM - 354 - 0147 - QFM - 5000 +		
	YN9 v G2LCP R - X496 +		
	G2LCP v YN9 R +		
0157	LANDED IFF "OFF"		
	OFF WATCH Davis		
	A1134 R1155 T1154 "OFF"		

Extract from Staff Wireless Operator Log

This log, shortened by half, shows that this was a night bombing exercise in Anson EF978 (crashed into the sea on 8th September 1943). Sergeant Travis checked the intercom, and IFF (Identification Friend or Foe) equipment, and switched this on after take off so that any of our night fighters which interrogated it would find the correct response. Communications are established between Llandwrog (code YN9) and the Anson (code G2LCP). The aircraft heads for Hell's Mouth bombing range and changes over to Penrhos control (code A7Y) shortly after 0120 hours. Bombing takes place just prior to 0126, after which a change back to Llandwrog control is made, followed by a request for the magnetic course to fly home. This QDM is given as 354 degrees at 0147 hours, and the Anson lands safely 10 minutes later.

Appendix D

Navigational Courses flown from No 9(O)AFU Penrhos and Llandwrog

Code No.	Route	Time
	Daytime Exercises	
M1	Basic map reading	2½ hrs
M2	Map reading and oblique photography. Various routes: ie. Base-Prestatyn-Kidderminster or Bridgnorth-Base	2½-3hrs
03(a)	Base-Maughold Head-(IoM)-Newton Stewart-Dalbeattie-Jurby-Bala-Base	2½ hrs
05(a)	Base-Penmon-Ayr-Base	2½ hrs
06(a)	Nav ex. Base-Llanerchymedd-Kirkcudbright-Base, or	2½ hrs
06(a)	Base-Llanerchymedd-Rhyl-Point of Ayr-Base.	2 hrs
07(a)	Base-Fairbourne-Aylesbury-Base	3 hrs
08(a)	Base-Penmon-Holywell-Stafford-Hereford-Tarporley-Penmon-Base	3 hrs
09(a)	Base-Cemaes Bay-Ballyquintin-Armagh-Moneymore-Ballyquintin-Base. (Map reading, Drift sights, Bearing compass, Astro compass, Oblique photography)	2½ hrs
011(a)	Base-Market Deeping-Banbury-Base	3 hrs
Plus	Sea exercises Square search Radius of action Air plot.	1-2hrs
	Night Flying Exercises Celestial navigation & radio bearings.	
NN2(b)	Base-Bardsey Island-Point Lynas-Base.	2½-3hrs
NO2	Base-Position 53.40N, 05.20W.,-Douglas Base	
NO6	Base-Cardigan-Fishguard-Chicken Rock-Douglas-Gt.Orme's Head-Base.	2½-3hrs
NO8	Base-Corsewall-Kirkcudbright-Douglas (Infra-Red)-Gt.Orme's Head-Conway-(Infra-Red)-Base	2½-3hrs
NO9	Base-Douglas-Shrewsbury-Allcott-Wrekin-Conway-Base	2½-3hrs
NO10	Base-Catterick-Carlisle-Isle of Man-Base	2½-3hrs

Note Many exercises were repeated for each trainee, who would fly initially as second navigator, and later as first navigator. These valuable extracts taken from Len Lambert's flying log.

Appendix E

Penrhos and Llandwrog Whitley and Anson Losses

Excluding those in Appendix A

Armstrong Whitworth Whitley

Date	Serial	Details	Casualties	
13.11.40	N1491	Crashed at Penrhos. Struck Fairey Battle on airfield	1K	4S
19.02.41	K7244	Ditched in Abersoch Bay after E/F. Recovered	2K	5S
24.06.41	K7247	Hit telegraph pole on approach to Penrhos, crashed on pyrotechnic store		8S
16.07.41	T4153	Crashed on delivery flight at Llandwrog		1S
10.10.41	K7252	Collided in circuit and crashed on Llandwrog airfield		
..	K9041	..	17K	
25.01.42	N1475	F/L after E/F onto headland by Porth Dinllaen		7S

Avro Anson

Date	Serial	Details	Casualties	
21.08.41	N9877	Crashed in sea descending through cloud nr Nevin	5K	
02.09.41	N9551	Hit sea in flight, ditched nr Aberdovey. Recovered		5S
24.10.41	N4884	Ditched after attempted F/L at night nr Fort Belan		5S
13.11.41	N9532	F/L on beach nr Bodorgan in bad weather		5S
06.01.42	N9822	Ditched 6m west Llanbedr		5S
09.05.42	N4922	Ditched 3m NW Llanddwyn Island		5S
10.06.42	N4983	Dived into sea on approach to Llandwrog	2K	
08.08.42	DJ125	Crashed in sea on take off from Llandwrog	4K	1S.
21.08.42	DJ117	Failed to return from night navigation exercise	5K	
22.08.42	R9639	Crashed in F/L at Tetchill, Salop	1K	4S
22.09.42	DJ126	Flew into Cairnsmore at night, off course	5K	
13.11.42	DJ628	Failed to return from night cross country flight	5K	
03.01.43	DJ619	Stalled on take off into sea 1m NE Llandwrog		5S
01.03.43	EG129	Dived into ground nr Penygroes after E/F at night	5K	
15.03.43	DJ627	F/L in sea off Anglesey after engine exploded		5S
29.03.43	DJ618	F/L in sea off Holyhead		5S
19.06.43	LT941	Crashed 1 mile north Penrhos		5S
28.07.43	DJ630	F/L at Ballyhalbert		5S
01.05.43	AX407	F/L in Irish Sea on night navigation exercise	5K	
15.08.43	LT485	F/L near Penrhos		5S
28.08.43	EF952	Struck house on approach to NE runway	2K	3S
04.09.43	EG278	Disintegrated in the air & crashed nr Caernarvon	4K	
08.09.43	EF978	Struck bank on take off and crashed into sea	1K	4S
10.10.43	EF820	Crashed into peat bog on Mull of Kintyre	5K	
25.03.44	DJ315	Struck high ground in cloud at Rhydwyn, Anglesey		5S
20.04.44	AX406	Hit tree in F/L at Bridge of Dee, Kirkcubright		5S
01.06.44	MG340	Overshot in bad weather & ditched off Llandwrog		5S
01.08.44	AW912	Ditched 80 yards NW Llandwrog airfield		5S
16.10.44	DJ621	Ditched Irish Sea after E/F 53 72N 04 58W		5S
18.12.44	EG218	F/L after EF on Trewan sands, Valley		5S
16.05.45	N9911	Crashed on landing in bad weather at RAF Mona	3K	2S

Appendix F

High Ground Aircraft Crashes in North and Mid Wales

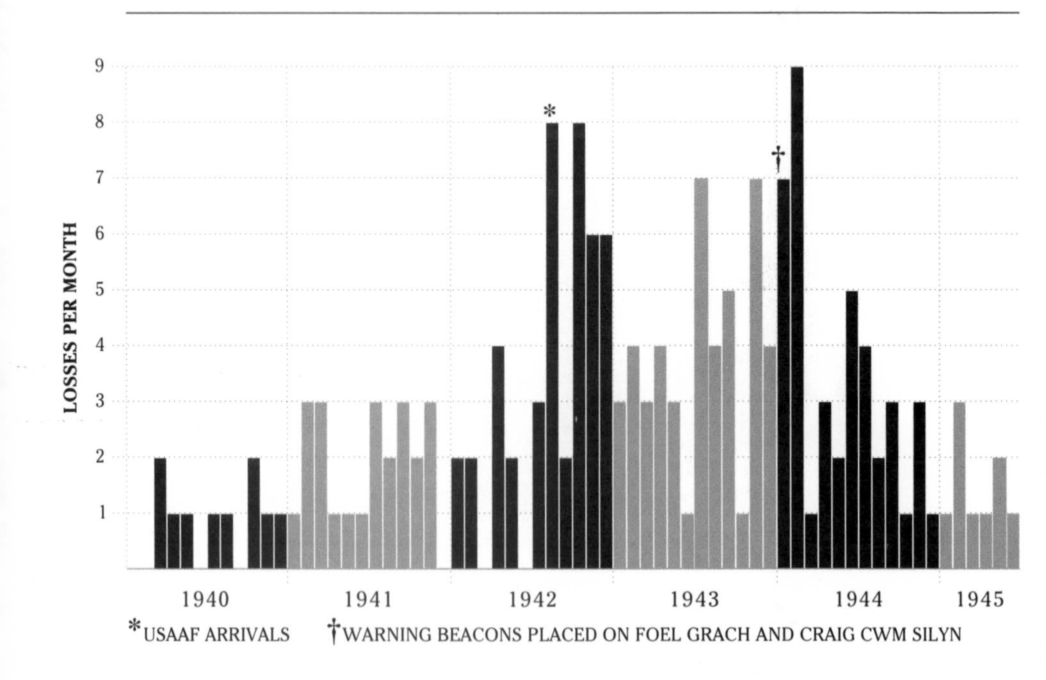

Epitaph

In the Commonwealth War Graves section of Llanbeblig Cemetery, Caernarfon, lies Pilot Officer J. M. Snow RAF, age 21, pilot of Anson N4983 which dived into the sea on approach to Llandwrog on 10th June 1942.

Etched on his headstone are these moving words.

TILL THE FUTURE
DARES FORGET THE PAST
HIS FATE AND FAME
SHALL BE AN ECHO AND A LIGHT
UNTO ETERNITY

Caernarfon Airport

Llandwrog has become Caernarfon Airport, so visitors can still find there that link with the past. The old flying control tower has been converted into a restaurant overlooking the airfield, with a strip alongside for visitors to picnic and observe aircraft movements. A large museum houses aircraft exhibits and a photographic display of the Llandwrog Mountain Rescue Team. Outside there is a fenced area for children with their own helicopter to play in, not to mention the beach nearby.